**Sports Illustrated Kids**

**Managing Editor** Mark Bechtel
**Creative Director** Beth Power Bugler
**Director of Photography** Marguerite Schropp Lucarelli
**Photo Editor** Annmarie Avila

**Created by 10Ten Media**

**Managing Directors** Bob Der, Scott Gramling, Ian Knowles
**Creative Director** Christian Rodriguez
**Managing Editor** Andrea Woo
**Senior Editor** Ed McGrogan
**Writers** Zachary Cohen, Phillip Crandall, Tim Gramling
**Reporter** Corinne Cummings

**Time Inc. Books**

**Publisher** Margot Schupf
**Vice President, Finance** Vandana Patel
**Executive Director, Marketing Services** Carol Pittard
**Executive Director, Business Development** Suzanne Albert
**Executive Director, Marketing** Susan Hettleman
**Publishing Director** Megan Pearlman
**Associate Director of Publicity** Courtney Greenhalgh
**Assistant General Counsel** Simone Procas
**Assistant Director, Special Sales** Ilene Schreider
**Assistant Director, Finance** Christine Font
**Senior Manager, Sales Marketing** Danielle Costa
**Senior Manager, Children's Category Marketing** Amanda Lipnick
**Senior Book Production Manager** Susan Chodakiewicz
**Associate Prepress Manager** Alex Voznesenskiy
**Associate Project Manager** Stephanie Braga

**Editorial Director** Stephen Koepp
**Art Director** Gary Stewart
**Senior Editors** Roe D'Angelo, Alyssa Smith
**Managing Editor** Matt DeMazza
**Editor, Children's Books** Jonathan White
**Copy Chief** Rina Bander
**Design Manager** Anne-Michelle Gallero
**Assistant Managing Editor** Gina Scauzillo
**Editorial Assistant** Courtney Mifsud

**Special thanks:** Allyson Angle, Katherine Barnet, Brad Beatson, Jeremy Biloon, John Champlin, Ian Chin, Rose Cirrincione, Assu Etsubneh, Mariana Evans, Alison Foster, Kristina Jutzi, David Kahn, Jean Kennedy, Hillary Leary, Samantha Long, Amy Mangus, Kimberly Marshall, Robert Martells, Nina Mistry, Melissa Presti, Danielle Prielipp, Kate Roncinske, Babette Ross, Dave Rozzelle, Matthew Ryan, Ricardo Santiago, Divyam Shrivastava

ISBN 10: 1-61893-134-2
ISBN 13: 978-1-61893-134-4
Library of Congress Control Number: 2015930326

Sports Illustrated Kids is a trademark of Time Inc.

We welcome your comments and suggestions about Sports Illustrated Kids Books.
Please write to us at:
Sports Illustrated Kids Books
Attention: Book Editors
P.O. Box 361095
Des Moines, IA 50336-1095

If you would like to order any of our hardcover Collector's Edition books, please call us at 1-800-327-6388 (Monday through Friday, 7 a.m. to 9 p.m. Central Time).

1 QGT 15

14

# Welcome

▶ Basketball is an exciting game filled with dunks, buzzer beaters, and thrilling plays made by the sport's biggest stars. This book features all the greats, from amazing shooters to sensational playmakers to imposing rebounders. Who was the youngest player to win the NBA MVP Award? Who has the most scoring titles in WNBA history? Find out the answers to those questions and more in this book of basketball's best players, both past and present.

# CONTENTS

112

92

78

35

CHAM

# PTONS

THESE PLAYERS LED
THEIR TEAMS TO THE ULTIMATE
PRIZE IN BASKETBALL

★ | SUPER STAT

# 20.9

MILES PER HOUR, THE SPEED AT
WHICH PARKER WAS CLOCKED
RUNNING IN 2012, THE FASTEST
EVER RECORDED IN
AN NBA GAME

# WHO WAS THE FIRST EUROPEAN-BORN PLAYER TO BE NAMED NBA FINALS MVP?

▶ When Gregg Popovich, the coach of the San Antonio Spurs, first heard about a 6' 2" guard from France named **Tony Parker**, he thought the same thing as most NBA executives: "Everybody knows you don't get point guards from Europe," he said, "because they're generally not quick enough and they don't have a grasp of the NBA game." But after watching film of Parker compete against promising U.S. players, Popovich was sold. The Spurs selected the 19-year-old with the 28th overall pick in the 2001 draft. Over the course of the next 13 seasons, Parker would win four NBA titles and become the first European-born player to be named Finals MVP.

In the fifth game after Parker's NBA debut — which made him the third Frenchman ever to play in an NBA game as well as the youngest player ever to suit up for the Spurs — he took over as the starting point guard. Playing alongside stars Tim Duncan and David Robinson, he led his team in assists (as well as steals) and made the All-Rookie team. Parker helped San Antonio win NBA championships in 2003 and '05, but it wasn't until the 2007 Finals that Parker really stole the spotlight. He shot 56.8% from the field and averaged 24.5 points, almost six points more than his regular season average that year, on his way to earning the Finals MVP award in a sweep of the Cleveland Cavaliers.

# Who was MVP of the first four WNBA Finals?

**Cynthia Cooper** is one of the greatest women's basketball players of all time, but the WNBA didn't exist when the two-time NCAA national champion finished her career at the University of Southern California. So in 1986, the guard took off for Europe, where she would lead Spanish and Italian leagues in scoring nine times over the next decade. Before the WNBA's inaugural 1997 season, Cooper, at the age of 34, signed on to play for the Houston Comets. She immediately established her dominance — Cooper won four Finals MVP awards while her team lost a total of only three playoff games. Cooper also led the WNBA in scoring her first three years and was named the regular season MVP her first two seasons.

**FAST FACT**

*BILL RUSSELL HAS THE MOST CHAMPIONSHIP RINGS IN NBA HISTORY. HE WON 11 WITH THE CELTICS.*

# Who had the most rebounds in an NBA Finals game?

Boston Celtics big man **Bill Russell** grabbed a record 40 rebounds in Game 2 of the 1960 Finals against the St. Louis Hawks, then matched that in a deciding 1962 Game 7 victory over the Los Angeles Lakers. Over his 13-year NBA career, he pulled down 21,620 rebounds, averaging 22.5 per game. He led the league in total rebounds four times. Since blocked shots were not tracked during the Celtics legend's career — and because the small things, such as setting picks, basket-to-basket foot speed, and fast-break passing, will always go unappreciated — rebounding may be the only stat that truly shows how dominant the five-time MVP was.

**42**

POINTS THAT JOHNSON SCORED IN THE CLINCHING GAME 6 OF THE 1980 NBA FINALS, THE MOST EVER BY A ROOKIE IN A FINALS GAME

# Who had the most triple doubles in the NBA Finals?

After a high school game in which Earvin Johnson had a triple double (36 points, 18 rebounds, and 16 assists), a local reporter gave him a nickname that would stick forever. **Magic Johnson** led Everett High School in Lansing, Michigan to a state title his senior year. His two triple doubles in the NCAA tournament two years later helped lead Michigan State to the 1979 NCAA title.

As a rookie with the Los Angeles Lakers, Johnson found himself in a position to win yet another championship. In Game 5 of the 1980 NBA Finals, with the series tied 2–2 against the Philadelphia 76ers, he had his first of seven Finals triple doubles, which is an NBA record. He had 14 points, 15 rebounds, and 10 assists in a 108–103 win, and the Lakers went on to win the title in six games. Johnson's last Finals triple double came in his last Finals game, against the Chicago Bulls in 1991.

**FAST FACT**

IN 2000, O'NEAL WAS NAMED MVP OF THE ALL-STAR GAME, THE NBA FINALS, AND THE REGULAR SEASON. HE BECAME THE THIRD PLAYER, AFTER WILLIS REED AND MICHAEL JORDAN, TO TAKE HOME ALL THREE HONORS IN THE SAME SEASON.

# WHO WAS THE LAST PLAYER TO WIN THREE STRAIGHT FINALS MVPs?

▶ **Shaquille O'Neal** didn't need much time to show that he was one of the greatest big men in the game. The Number 1 pick of the 1992 draft, he won Rookie of the Year with the Orlando Magic and led the team to the Finals the following season. He joined the Los Angeles Lakers in 1996, but the team failed to reach the NBA Finals in any of O'Neal's first three seasons there. That's when L.A. brought in legendary coach Phil Jackson.

Jackson told the 7' 1" Shaq there was no reason he couldn't become an MVP if he worked hard enough, and in 1999–2000, he did exactly that. The Lakers beat the Indiana Pacers in a Finals series in which O'Neal was the leading scorer in all six games, making him an easy pick for Finals MVP. The following year, the Lakers swept all three playoff series in the Western Conference and lost only one Finals game to the Philadelphia 76ers on their way to earning their second straight title. It was an extremely physical match-up against 76ers star center Dikembe Mutombo, but O'Neal averaged 33 points, 15.8 rebounds, 4.8 assists, and 3.4 blocks to earn his second Finals MVP award. Another dominating NBA Finals in 2002 — this time, a four-game sweep of the New Jersey Nets — gave L.A. its three-peat and Shaq a third Finals MVP honor.

# Who was the first teenager to be the Number 1 overall pick in a WNBA draft?

**Lauren Jackson** 's parents were both basketball stars who played for Australia's national teams. (Her mother also set scoring and rebounding records at LSU.) So it's no surprise that Jackson quickly became a star on the court, as well as the first teenager to be taken with the Number 1 overall pick in the WNBA draft.

As a 16-year-old with excellent shooting range, post play, and ball control, Jackson was the youngest player ever on Australia's national team. She helped her country win a bronze medal at the 1998 World Championships and a silver at the 2000 Olympics, where the 6' 5" phenom led the team in points and rebounds. In 2001, the Seattle Storm chose the 19-year-old with the top pick of the draft. Jackson made an immediate impression — she led rookies in scoring, rebounding, steals, and blocks. She would go on to win three MVP awards and lead Seattle to two championships.

★ **SUPER STAT**

# 575

CAREER POINTS THAT JACKSON SCORED IN FOUR TRIPS TO THE OLYMPICS, A WOMEN'S RECORD

# Who was the last Detroit Piston to be named NBA Finals MVP?

**Chauncey Billups** joined the Detroit Pistons in 2002, his sixth team in six seasons. Each stint had its own unique circumstances — including one in Orlando where a shoulder injury prevented Billups from ever suiting up — but with each situation, the guard never found solid ground to get his career going. When Detroit's President of Basketball Operations Joe Dumars (a former Pistons player whose Number 4 jersey inspired Billups to wear that number in college) told Billups that the Pistons were committed to him leading the team, Billups finally felt comfortable. In the 2003–04 NBA Finals, with a team that lacked a star, Billups averaged 21 points — more than four points higher than his regular season average — and played stellar defense to beat the Los Angeles Lakers in five games and earn the Finals MVP award.

## FAST FACT

BILLUPS EARNED THE NICKNAME MR. BIG SHOT FOR HIS CLUTCH SHOOTING DURING THE PISTONS' TITLE RUN.

# WHO HAD THE MOST PLAYOFF DOUBLE DOUBLES IN NBA HISTORY?

▶ On June 12, 2014 — the same night he broke Kareem Abdul-Jabbar's record for most playoff minutes played — **Tim Duncan** scored 10 points and pulled down 11 rebounds to help the San Antonio Spurs defeat the Miami Heat in Game 4 of the NBA Finals. It wasn't the flashiest stat line of his career, but it was enough for the power forward to earn a record-breaking 158th playoff double double. That's almost two full extra seasons' worth of everyday scoring and rebounding consistency, which earned Duncan the equally non-flashy nickname the Big Fundamental.

Duncan has had a calm, businesslike demeanor since his college days at Wake Forest University, where he was a two-time All-America and the college player of the year in 1997. The Number 1 pick of the 1997 draft, Duncan went on to win Rookie of the Year and make the first of 14 All-Star Games. Duncan has said that one reason he doesn't show any emotion is because displaying frustration or disappointment would give his opponents an advantage. Perhaps the only thing he is better known for than consistency is the dominance that comes from it. Duncan has collected the Finals MVP award three of the five times the Spurs have won the title, and was only two blocks away from earning a quadruple double in the clinching Game 6 of the 2003 NBA Finals. When told how close he was to achieving that feat, which has occurred only four times in NBA history, he simply responded, "That's cool."

★ SUPER STAT

**11** OF 16 POSTSEASONS IN WHICH DUNCAN HAS AVERAGED A DOUBLE DOUBLE, GIVING HIM A CAREER PLAYOFF AVERAGE OF 21.3 POINTS AND 11.7 REBOUNDS

## FAST FACT

GROWING UP, DUNCAN WAS AN ELITE SWIMMER. HE STOPPED COMPETING AFTER HURRICANE HUGO DESTROYED HIS TEAM'S POOL IN 1989.

15

# Who scored the most points in one quarter of an NBA Finals game?

In 1988, the Detroit Pistons were up three games to two against the Los Angeles Lakers in the NBA Finals, but found themselves down 56–48 in the third quarter of Game 6. That's when guard **Isiah Thomas** took over, scoring the next 14 points. All of a sudden, on a fast break, Thomas crumpled to the ground with a sprained ankle. Thomas was hurt, but with the Lakers resurging, he hobbled off the bench and added another 11 points, setting a Finals record with 25 for the quarter. That gave Detroit the lead going into the fourth. Thomas finished with 43 points, six steals, a poked eye, a jammed finger, and the sprained ankle. The one shot he couldn't make was a game-winner in the final minute, as the Pistons would lose both that game and the series.

**FAST FACT**

*MIKAN WAS SO DOMINANT THAT THE NBA HAD TO MAKE RULE CHANGES, SUCH AS ADDING A SHOT CLOCK.*

# Who was the first NBA player enshrined in the Hall of Fame?

Six-foot-ten **George Mikan** was the first game-changing big man in the NBA. When the league formed in 1949, it took teams from the NBL and BAA, both of which Mikan had dominated for three seasons. (He led his teams to championships each of those seasons.) Mikan's Minneapolis Lakers would win the first NBA title in 1950, anchored by his average of 31.3 points in the playoffs. He won three more championships over the course of his short six-season career in the NBA. When the Hall of Fame inducted its first class in 1959, Mikan was an obvious choice.

# Who was the only person to win MVP and Coach of the Year in the NBA?

Before he was regarded as one of the best shooting forwards ever, and before he had demonstrated enough wisdom to lead a team from the sidelines as a coach, **Larry Bird** drove a garbage truck. It was one of many community jobs the Indiana native took on after leaving college due to homesickness. He gave school another chance a year later, and after he was drafted by the Boston Celtics in 1978, Bird quickly became an all-time great. In his 13-year career, he was named NBA MVP three times and won three championship rings. The 12-time All-Star retired in 1992 and swore coaching wasn't for him, but in 1997 a job opening with his hometown Indiana Pacers proved too tempting to resist. In 1998, he won Coach of the Year as his Pacers improved by 19 wins from the previous season. As Pacers' President of Basketball Operations, Bird was named Executive of the Year in 2012. He is the only person to win awards in so many areas of the game.

★ | **SUPER STAT**

**3** CONSECUTIVE MVP AWARDS WON BY BIRD (1983-84, '84-85, '85-86), MAKING HIM ONE OF THREE PLAYERS – ALONG WITH BILL RUSSELL AND WILT CHAMBERLAIN – TO TAKE HOME THE AWARD IN THREE STRAIGHT SEASONS

# WHO WAS THE FIRST FATHER-SON PAIR TO BOTH WIN MULTIPLE NBA CHAMPIONSHIPS?

Bill Walton

▶ **Luke Walton** 's earliest memories were going to Boston Garden to watch his father, **Bill** , play. (That, and going to Celtics practices, where he was dared by players such as Larry Bird to squirt shaving cream into other people's shoes.) Had Luke gone to every Boston home game in 1985–86, the five-year-old would have seen only one Celtics loss all year, as his often-injured father put together a memorable comeback season to win the Sixth Man of the Year award. Bill also scored a then-season-high 20 points on the night of Luke's sixth birthday. The Celtics won the NBA title that season, giving the center a second championship ring to go along with the one he earned with the 1977 Portland Trail Blazers.

It's only fitting that Bill, considered one of the best all-around players when he was healthy, would have four sons who also played the sport at an elite level. All four made Division I college teams, and Luke would be a successful NBA player. Drafted in 2003 by the Los Angeles Lakers, he won championships with L.A. in 2009 and '10. Still, nothing came easy as Bill's kid, particularly since his father was still a part of the game as a TV commentator. "It used to get awkward in film sessions when we'd watch film and my dad would be saying some critical things about my teammates," Luke once said. "But he'd say critical things about me, too. I wasn't even his son. He'd call me 'Walton.'"

Luke Walton

**FAST FACT**

IN COLLEGE, BILL WALTON HELPED UCLA WIN NATIONAL CHAMPIONSHIPS IN 1972 AND '73. THE BRUINS WENT UNDEFEATED IN BOTH SEASONS.

# Who was the first player to win MVP, Finals MVP, and DPOY in the same season?

Growing up in Nigeria, **Hakeem Olajuwon** played handball and soccer and didn't pick up a basketball until he was a teenager. But he proved to be a natural in the sport. Agile and nearly seven feet tall when the Houston Rockets drafted him in 1984, Olajuwon became famous for his moves and shakes, as he incorporated head fakes and fleet footwork. No season showcased his talents better than 1993–94, when he won the league MVP and the Defensive Player of the Year awards. In a critical Game 6 against the New York Knicks in the NBA Finals, Hakeem the Dream blocked a potentially game-winning three-pointer as the clock ran out. Then in Game 7, he scored a game-high 25 points to go along with 10 rebounds as Houston won its first-ever title. Olajuwon was named Finals MVP and was the first player to win those three major awards in the same season.

★ **SUPER STAT**

**6** TIMES THAT OLAJUWON HAD A FIVE-BY-FIVE GAME (IN WHICH A PLAYER HAS AT LEAST FIVE POINTS, REBOUNDS, ASSISTS, STEALS, AND BLOCKS), THE MOST SINCE THOSE STATS WERE KEPT

*WORTHY HAS THE THIRD-MOST STEALS IN LAKERS FRANCHISE HISTORY BEHIND MAGIC JOHNSON AND KOBE BRYANT.*

# Who had the only triple double in an NBA Finals Game 7 victory?

Expectations were high when the Los Angeles Lakers drafted **James Worthy** with the first pick in 1982. After all, he had been an All-America at North Carolina, winning the Most Outstanding Player at the 1982 NCAA tournament following a 28-point performance in the title game. The Lakers would win championships in 1985 and '87 with help from Worthy's playoff average of more than 20 points per game, but it was in the 1988 Finals against the Detroit Pistons in which his biggest contribution came. In a tight Game 7 victory, Worthy had 36 points, 16 rebounds, and 10 assists for the only triple double ever in a Game 7 of the Finals. Worthy would earn the Finals MVP and become known as Big Game James.

# Who led her team to the first back-to-back championships in women's NCAA history?

**Cheryl Miller** was a larger-than-life phenom in high school, breaking points records and once scoring 105 points. As a college freshman, she led the University of Southern California to the 1982–83 NCAA title game against defending champion Louisiana Tech, which had won 30 straight games. Miller scored 27 points with nine rebounds, four blocks, and four steals in a victory. She won Most Outstanding Player, an honor she'd reclaim the next year when USC beat Tennessee for its second straight title to become the first back-to-back women's champions.

# WHO HAD THE HIGHEST SCORING AVERAGE IN NBA PLAYOFF HISTORY?

▶ **Michael Jordan** didn't make his high school varsity basketball team his sophomore year. While that's a shock, since he is known as one of the greatest players of all time, it is also one reason he became so dominant. As Jordan said during his 2009 Hall of Fame speech, not making that team turned him into a focused competitor with something to prove. In the 1985–86 season, Jordan's second year in the NBA, he led his Chicago Bulls to a playoff matchup against the Boston Celtics, which had lost only one home game all season. In Game 2, Jordan lit up for 63 points, the most ever in a playoff game. Two years later, Jordan put up back-to-back 50-point games as the Bulls beat the Cleveland Cavaliers. With his team trailing early in Game 1 of the 1992 Finals, Jordan scored 33 points in 17 minutes and broke the playoff record for threes in a single half. In the 1993 Finals, he averaged a Finals-record 41 points per game. Add it all up, and Jordan's playoff-record scoring average (33.4 points) is higher than his regular-season-record scoring average (30.1).

**FAST FACT**

*JORDAN BRIEFLY LEFT BASKETBALL AFTER THE BULLS' THIRD TITLE. HE WENT TO PLAY BASEBALL FOR THE CHICAGO WHITE SOX'S DOUBLE-A TEAM AND FINISHED THE 1994 SEASON WITH 30 STOLEN BASES.*

# Who was the only U.S. Naval Academy graduate to win an NBA title?

In 1983, **David Robinson** took his excellent grades and single year of basketball-playing experience to the Navy. At 6' 8" he was taller than the Academy's height limit, but Robinson was given a special exception that allowed him to stay. He eventually grew to 7' 1" and became the top pick in the 1987 draft. Robinson soon proved to be one of the most respected big men to play the game. The Admiral spent his entire career with the San Antonio Spurs, winning the MVP award in 1995 and two NBA titles, in 1999 and 2003.

★ | SUPER STAT

**71** POINTS THAT ROBINSON SCORED ON APRIL 24, 1994, MAKING HIM ONE OF FIVE PLAYERS WITH MORE THAN 70 POINTS IN A GAME

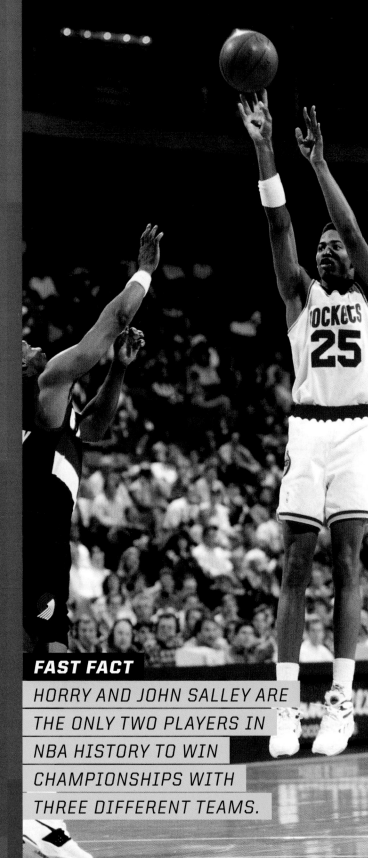

# Who earned the nickname Big Shot Bob for his clutch shooting in the playoffs?

The Houston Rockets traded **Robert Horry** to Detroit in 1994, believing the second-year forward was relying on superstar Hakeem Olajuwon too much instead of shooting the ball himself. As Horry was getting dressed for his first game in the Pistons' locker room, he learned that the trade had fallen through, and he'd be returning to Houston. He kept that Pistons jersey as a reminder never to hesitate and to take the shot. And though he never became a scoring leader in the league, his knack for finding the net when it really mattered became his trademark. In seven Finals series during his career — two with the Rockets, three with the Lakers, and two with the Spurs — Big Shot Bob hit a total of 53 three-pointers. Some were open shots mid-game, some were unforgettable clutch threes with only seconds left, but all of them added up to a Finals record, a cool nickname, and, most notably, seven championship rings.

## FAST FACT

*HORRY AND JOHN SALLEY ARE THE ONLY TWO PLAYERS IN NBA HISTORY TO WIN CHAMPIONSHIPS WITH THREE DIFFERENT TEAMS.*

# WHO WAS FINALS MVP WHEN THE CELTICS WON THEIR TITLE IN 2008?

▶ **Paul Pierce** grew up a die-hard fan of the Los Angeles Lakers, whose archrival in the 1980s were the Boston Celtics. But when Boston drafted Pierce in 1998, his allegiance shifted and he didn't take long to impress, scoring 19 points and grabbing nine rebounds in his first game.

In preparation for the 2007–08 season, the Celtics made two huge trades, bringing in Kevin Garnett and Ray Allen to team Pierce with players who could do damage in the playoffs. They made it all the way to the NBA Finals that year — and who should they meet there but the Lakers. In the third quarter of Game 1, Pierce injured his knee and needed to be carried off the court and put in a wheelchair. But he eventually returned and hit two three-pointers in 22 seconds to give his team the lead and a Game 1 victory. Over a tough six-game series, Pierce averaged 21.8 points, 4.5 rebounds, and 6.3 assists. His performance lead Boston to its first title since 1986 and earned him the Finals MVP award.

## FAST FACT

PIERCE WON THE 2010 THREE-POINT SHOOTOUT DURING THE ALL-STAR WEEKEND, BECOMING THE FIRST CELTICS PLAYER SINCE LARRY BIRD TO WIN THE CONTEST.

★ SUPER STAT

**2,144**

POINTS SCORED BY PIERCE IN 2001-02, THE MOST IN THE NBA THAT SEASON

# COOL
# CHARA

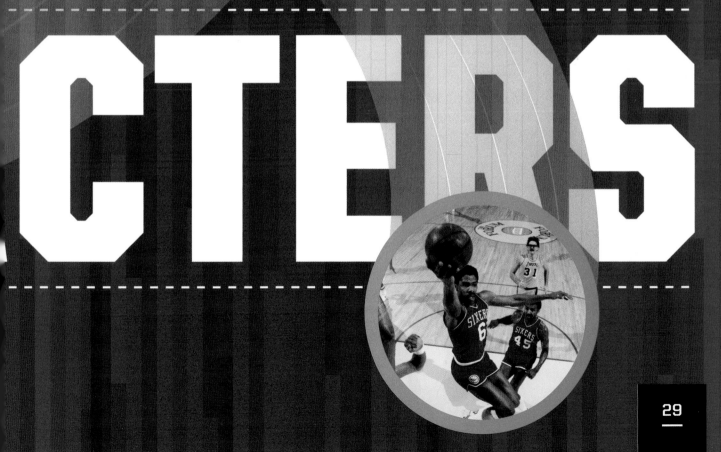

★ THESE PLAYERS LEFT THEIR MARK ON AND OFF THE COURT ➤

# CTERS

# WHO INSPIRED "FEAR THE BEARD" SIGNS AT GAMES?

**37** POINTS SCORED BY HARDEN IN HIS HOUSTON ROCKETS DEBUT, ON OCTOBER 31, 2012, TIED FOR THE SECOND-MOST EVER BY A PLAYER IN HIS FIRST GAME WITH A NEW TEAM

▶ When he was a sophomore at Arizona State, **James Harden** decided he wasn't going to shave anymore. Since then, opposing players have had plenty of reason to "fear the beard." Harden is one of basketball's most savvy scorers. He's a great ball-handler with an uncanny feel for getting defenders off-balance. And his lefthanded shooting stroke is one of the prettiest in the NBA.

Harden was an All-America player in 2008–09, and in '09 was drafted third overall by the Oklahoma City Thunder. He proved to be the missing piece for the Thunder, who had young stars in Kevin Durant and Russell Westbrook but had not made the playoffs since relocating to Oklahoma City from Seattle. In 2009–10, the Thunder made the playoffs, and Harden quickly developed into one of the game's best scorers. In 2011–12, he won NBA Sixth Man of the Year honors and helped the Thunder reach the NBA Finals. Unable to afford new contracts for all their young stars, Oklahoma City traded Harden to the Houston Rockets. In Houston, his beard continued to grow along with his stardom. A starter for the first time, Harden was named an All-Star in each of his first three seasons in Houston.

**FAST FACT**

THE THIRD OVERALL PICK IN 2009, HARDEN BECAME THE FIRST PLAYER EVER DRAFTED BY THE OKLAHOMA CITY THUNDER. THE TEAM HAD RELOCATED FROM SEATTLE AFTER THE 2008 DRAFT.

# Who was known as the Iceman?

His calm, cool demeanor and his incredible skills on the court made the Iceman the perfect nickname for **George Gervin**.

Gervin, a 6' 7" swingman who often attacked from the perimeter, was a terrific scorer. His go-to shot was the finger roll. Gervin would glide toward the basket and sink finger rolls from as far out as the free-throw line. Gervin played most of his career with the San Antonio Spurs, winning four scoring titles and making nine All-Star teams.

Early in the 1981–82 season, Gervin missed a week of games while nursing a thigh injury. His replacement, Ron Brewer, scored 39, 40, and 44 points in the three games Gervin missed. In his first game back, Gervin scored 47 points. Afterward, Gervin was asked if his play was motivated by possibly losing his starting job. His answer? "Ice be cool."

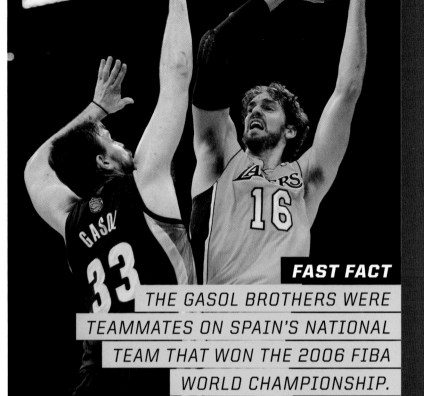

**FAST FACT**

THE GASOL BROTHERS WERE TEAMMATES ON SPAIN'S NATIONAL TEAM THAT WON THE 2006 FIBA WORLD CHAMPIONSHIP.

# Who were the only brothers to be traded for each other?

After winning three straight titles from 1999–2000 through 2001–02, the Los Angeles Lakers went into a championship drought. So midway through the '07–08 season, L.A. made a blockbuster trade for an All-Star big man: they acquired **Pau Gasol** from the Memphis Grizzlies. In return, the Grizzlies got two first-round picks, some young players, and a former Lakers second-round pick who had been playing in Europe. That player had a familiar name: **Marc Gasol**. Pau and Marc are the only brothers in the NBA ever to be traded for each other.

The trade ended up benefiting both teams. In Pau's first three seasons with the Lakers, they went to the NBA Finals three times, winning it twice. Meanwhile, Marc, a 7-footer, developed into an All-Star for the Grizzlies and won NBA Defensive Player of the Year honors in '12–13.

# Who was the shortest player in NBA history?

It's difficult for a small player to contribute in the NBA, which is why it was so amazing that **Muggsy Bogues** played for 14 seasons. At 5' 3", he is the shortest player to ever play in the league. Bogues starred in college at Wake Forest University, where his No. 14 jersey is retired. He won the Frances Pomeroy Naismith Award, given to the most outstanding senior who is 6' 0" or shorter, for the 1986–87 season.

Bogues went on to become an excellent playmaker at the NBA level. He played his rookie season with the Washington Bullets, who drafted him 12th overall in 1987. They did not protect his rights, however, so he ended up heading to the Charlotte Hornets in the 1988 expansion draft. Bogues went on to be a longtime starter for the Hornets. He had two seasons in which he averaged more than 10 assists per game and was a pest on defense with 1.5 steals per game over the course of his career.

★ **SUPER STAT**

**39** CAREER BLOCKS MADE BY THE PINT-SIZED BOGUES, INCLUDING A REMARKABLE ONE ON A SHOT ATTEMPTED BY 7' 0" BIG MAN PATRICK EWING

# Who was the tallest player in NBA history?

**Gheorghe Muresan** was listed at 7' 7", making him the tallest player in the history of the NBA. Manute Bol was also listed at that height, but it is widely believed that Muresan had at least a half an inch over him. Muresan was drafted by the Washington Bullets in the second round of the 1993 NBA draft. Muresan played only five years in the NBA, but he was a very effective player when he stayed healthy. Over the course of his career, he blocked 1.5 shots per game. In 1995–96, he blocked 2.3 shots per game while averaging 14.5 points and 9.6 rebounds with a 58.4% shooting percentage from the field. He was the NBA's Most Improved Player that season. Muresan continued to play professional basketball overseas after his NBA career came to an end.

## FAST FACT

MURESAN STARRED ALONGSIDE ACTOR BILLY CRYSTAL IN THE 1998 FILM MY GIANT.

# Who was known as Dr. J?

When **Julius Erving** was playing basketball at Roosevelt High School in New York, he and friend Leon Saunders had nicknames for each other. Erving called Saunders the Professor, and Saunders called Erving the Doctor. Soon, everyone started calling him Dr. Julius, which was shortened to Dr. J.

A 6' 7" swingman, Erving would glide to the basket and, with his incredible vertical leap, hang in the air. Playing for the University of Massachusetts, he averaged an amazing 26.3 points and 20.2 rebounds in two seasons. He joined the ABA's New York Nets in 1973 and went on to win the league's MVP award three times while leading the Nets to two championships.

After the ABA merged with the NBA for the 1976–77 season, the Philadelphia 76ers bought out Erving's contract, and Dr. J became a star in Philly. He was the league's Most Valuable Player in 1980–81 and led Philly to a title in '82–83.

★ **SUPER STAT**

# 30,026

CAREER POINTS FOR ERVING BETWEEN THE NBA AND ABA, MAKING HIM SIXTH ALL TIME ON THE NBA-ABA SCORING LIST

# WHO WAS THE FIRST FEMALE PLAYER TO HAVE A NIKE SHOE NAMED AFTER HER?

▶ Playing college basketball at Texas Tech, **Sheryl Swoopes** burst onto the national scene with one of the greatest big-game performances ever. She led the Lady Raiders to the 1993 NCAA title by scoring 47 points in the final, the most ever in a men's or women's title game. A 6-foot forward, she was skilled, gritty, and aggressive on the court.

But there was no U.S. professional league for her to compete in after that season. It wasn't until 1996 when the WNBA was born that Swoopes joined the Houston Comets as the league's first player. She took the court midway through the season, six weeks after giving birth to her son.

Swoopes had another first in '96: She became the first female player to have a Nike signature shoe. Swoopes helped the Comets win the WNBA championship in each of the league's first four years. She played in the league into her 40s, making six All-Star game appearances and becoming the league's first three-time MVP.

★ SUPER STAT

# 657

CAREER STEALS MADE BY SWOOPES, THIRD-MOST ON THE WNBA'S ALL-TIME LIST

## FAST FACT

PLAYING FOR THE COMETS ON JULY 27, 1999, SWOOPES RECORDED THE FIRST TRIPLE DOUBLE IN WNBA HISTORY: 14 POINTS, 15 REBOUNDS, 10 ASSISTS AGAINST THE DETROIT SHOCK.

# Who was the lockdown defender who earned the nickname the Glove?

An electrifying point guard for the Seattle SuperSonics in the 1990s, **Gary Payton** was known for his intense playing style and his big mouth (he loved to talk trash). But more than anything, he was known for his tenacious defense.

During the 1993 Western Conference Finals, Payton's Sonics faced off against the Phoenix Suns. Phoenix had a star point guard of its own: Kevin Johnson. The two were locked in a fierce battle, and Payton's defense was clearly bothering Johnson. According to Payton, after Game 4 his cousin told him he was "holding Johnson like a baseball in a glove." And with that, one of the NBA's great nicknames was born.

Payton was the NBA Defensive Player of the Year in 1995–96. In the 1996 Finals, he guarded Michael Jordan and held him to 23 points in Game 4, Jordan's lowest output in a Finals game at that point. In Game 6, he held Jordan to 22 points.

**FAST FACT**

PAYTON WAS ALSO AN OFFENSIVE STAR. HE IS THE SONICS' ALL-TIME LEADING SCORER.

★ | SUPER STAT

**5**

CONSECUTIVE SEASONS IN
WHICH WEBBER AVERAGED
20 POINTS AND
10 REBOUNDS FOR
THE KINGS

## Who led the Sacramento Kings to their only 60-win season?

Before the NBA, **Chris Webber** was the leader of the University of Michigan's famous Fab Five team. In 1991–92, he and four other freshmen made up the starting lineup for Michigan. Known for their exciting play and unique style, the Fab Five made two national title game appearances.

After strong seasons with the Golden State Warriors and Washington Wizards to start his NBA career, Webber flourished in Sacramento. The Kings let him run their offense from the "high post." An accomplished scorer but also an outstanding passer, he averaged 20 points, 13 rebounds, and 4.1 assists in his first season with the Kings, leading them to the playoffs.

Behind Webber, Sacramento became a power in the Western Conference. It finished the 2001–02 season with the NBA's best record (61–21). After his retirement, the Kings retired Webber's Number 4 jersey.

## Who was the first woman signed to an NBA contract?

When she was a senior at Sonora High School in La Habra, California, **Ann Meyers** became the only high schooler to play for the U.S. national team. The 5'9" guard was so dominant that UCLA offered her a full athletic scholarship for its women's basketball team, the first the school had ever given to a female athlete. Playing for the Bruins, Meyers became the first player in history, male or female, to be named to the Kodak All-America team four straight years. She was so good that on September 5, 1980, the Indiana Pacers signed her to a $50,000 contract. Meyers had a three-day tryout with the team, though in the end she didn't make the cut. But Meyers had plenty of success playing professionally — she was the first player drafted into the Women's Professional Basketball League (WPBL) and was named co-MVP in '79–80.

# WHO HAD A TRIPLE DOUBLE IN 20 MINUTES OF PLAYING TIME DURING THE 2013-14 SEASON?

▶ Anyone who has ever watched an Oklahoma City Thunder game knows that **Russell Westbrook** is fast. From the moment he stepped on the court in the Thunder's first-ever game in 2008, the 6' 3" point guard has been a blur with the ball in his hands. His speed and fearless attacking style have made him one of the top point guards in the NBA.

When the Thunder hosted the Philadelphia 76ers on March 4, 2014, Westbrook piled up statistics with amazing speed. He fed teammate Serge Ibaka for a lay-up 11 seconds into the game. He went on to pile up assists, points, and rebounds as the Thunder cruised to an easy victory. Because the Thunder led by more than 20 points early in the second half, Westbrook played only 20 minutes and 17 seconds, sitting the entire fourth quarter. But that was enough time for him to collect 13 points, 10 rebounds, and 14 assists, the second-fastest triple double ever recorded in the NBA. (The fastest was the Syracuse Nationals' Jim Tucker, who had 12 points, 10 rebounds, and 10 assists in a game in 1955.)

Westbrook has complemented his furious style on the court with some wacky fashion off of it. His postgame outfits have become must-see, from colorful horn-rimmed glasses to wild-patterned shirts.

**FAST FACT**
*WESTBROOK PLAYED COLLEGE BASKETBALL AT UCLA, ALONGSIDE FELLOW NBA ALL-STAR KEVIN LOVE.*

★ SUPER STAT

# 439

CONSECUTIVE GAMES (REGULAR SEASON AND PLAYOFFS) IN WHICH WESTBROOK PLAYED TO START HIS NBA CAREER

# WHO WAS THE TALLEST PLAYER TO APPEAR IN AN NBA ALL-STAR GAME?

▶ The NBA had seen giants like the 7' 6" **Yao Ming** before: Gheorghe Muresan (7' 7"), Manute Bol (7' 7"), and Shawn Bradley (7' 6"). All of them were role players in the NBA — but Yao was different. The top pick of the 2002 NBA draft out of China, Yao had the kind of athleticism, strength, and coordination rarely seen in 7-footers.

Yao didn't score a single point in his NBA debut. But a few weeks later he started piling up points, 20 against the Los Angeles Lakers and 30 against the Dallas Mavericks. By midseason he was a double-double machine and was elected to start the All-Star game as a rookie, the tallest player ever to play in the game. Yao made the All-Star team in each of his eight NBA seasons.

But with the Chinese national team running him through a grueling schedule every offseason, he missed the entire 2009–10 NBA season with a foot injury. He tried to come back a year later, but was forced to retire after just five games. His NBA career wasn't long, but it was great.

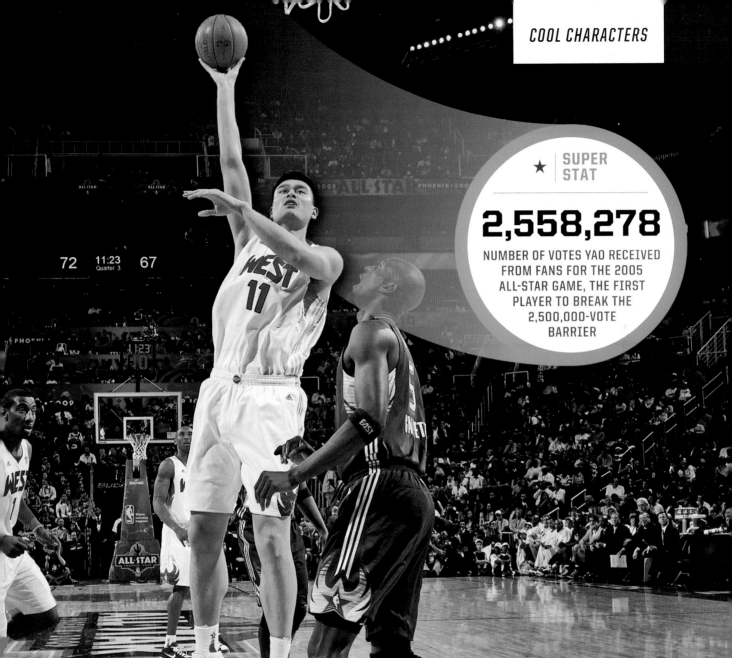

★ **SUPER STAT**

## 2,558,278

NUMBER OF VOTES YAO RECEIVED FROM FANS FOR THE 2005 ALL-STAR GAME, THE FIRST PLAYER TO BREAK THE 2,500,000-VOTE BARRIER

**FAST FACT**

YAO SCORED ONLY 20 POINTS TOTAL IN HIS FIRST SIX NBA GAMES. HE FINISHED HIS NBA CAREER WITH AN AVERAGE OF 19 POINTS PER GAME.

# Who was the shortest Slam Dunk Contest winner?

Over the years, the NBA's Slam Dunk Contest has showcased some of basketball's most dynamic players performing the game's most exciting play. And in 1986, it brought one of the most surprising moments in sports history. In a game dominated by big men, 5' 7" **Spud Webb** took home the Slam Dunk title.

At the All-Star weekend in Dallas, defending Slam Dunk champ Dominique Wilkins of the Atlanta Hawks was expected to retain his title. Instead, his pint-sized teammate stole the show.

When the two Hawks got to the finals, Webb wowed the judges by bouncing a high lob to himself, and finishing with a reverse dunk. The title was his.

While Webb is best known for his dunk title, he had a solid all-around career. He was an important role player off the bench for a Hawks team that often contended in the Eastern Conference. Later in his career he played for the Sacramento Kings, averaging more than seven assists per game in back-to-back seasons.

**FAST FACT**

WEBB WAS A JUDGE AT THE 2010 SLAM DUNK CONTEST IN DALLAS, THE FIRST TIME IT HAD BEEN HELD IN THAT CITY SINCE HIS WIN IN 1986.

★ **SUPER STAT**

**2** WADE TROPHIES WON BY LIEBERMAN, ONE OF THREE WOMEN TO WIN THE AWARD AS THE NCAA'S TOP FEMALE BASKETBALL PLAYER MULTIPLE TIMES

## Who was the oldest player in the history of the WNBA?

Along with an uncanny ability to score, Nancy Lieberman had unmatched ball-handling and passing skills. She was a three-time All-America at Old Dominion University and helped anchor a U.S. team that won a silver medal at the 1976 Montreal Olympics and gold at the 1979 world championships. Lieberman was also the first woman to play in a men's professional game, competing for the Springfield Fame of the United States Basketball League in 1986.

Lieberman was in the twilight of her career when the WNBA was formed in 1997. In the league's first season, she suited up for the Phoenix Mercury as the league's oldest player (age 39). She retired and went into coaching after that season, but came back for one more stint — 11 years later. At age 50, the Hall of Famer played for the Detroit Shock for one game, finishing with two assists.

## Who was the only player with more blocked shots than points in an NBA career?

In the 1983 draft, the San Diego Clippers picked Manute Bol despite the fact that they had never seen him play. Why? Because the center from Sudan was 7' 7" tall!

Bol never played for San Diego — he was declared ineligible for the draft — but two years later, the Washington Bullets selected him in the second round. Bol went on to play 10 seasons in the NBA, mostly as a back up. Despite being very thin, his height made him a defensive force. He blocked 15 shots in a game twice, and blocked eight shots in a quarter twice, tying an NBA record. Bol finished his career with 2,086 blocks, far more than the number of points he scored (1,599).

★ **SUPER STAT**

**20** LETTERS IN GIANNIS ANTETOKOUNMPO'S NAME, THE LONGEST NON-HYPHENATED FULL NAME FOR AN NBA FIRST-ROUND PICK SINCE CLARENCE WEATHERSPOON IN 1992

# WHO IS KNOWN AS THE GREEK FREAK?

▶ As soon as **Giannis Antetokounmpo** was drafted 15th overall by the Milwaukee Bucks in the 2013 draft, it was clear he would need a nickname. His name is not easy to pronounce (YAHN-iss Ah-deh-toh-KOON-boh). Why is the "Greek Freak" the perfect nickname?

Antetokounmpo, the son of Nigerian immigrants, grew up in Greece. That's the "Greek" part of his nickname. As for the "Freak" part, consider this: Antetokounmpo spent the summer of 2014 preparing to become a point guard. He's quick, a strong ball-handler, and has a really good feel for passing. But he isn't your typical point guard. Antetokounmpo is 6' 11", and he might still be growing. He could be the league's first 7-foot point guard.

As a rookie in 2013–14, Antetokounmpo made some jaw-dropping plays. Once, against the Philadelphia 76ers, he turned the ball over, then hustled back to block a lay-up at the last moment, tumbling to the ground out of bounds. Another Sixers player grabbed the rebound, and the Greek Freak got up off the floor, ran back in bounds, and blocked his lay-up too.

Only time will tell whether Antetokounmpo will become a star. But one thing is already clear: The Greek Freak is one-of-a-kind.

**FAST FACT**

ANTETOKOUNMPO'S OLDER BROTHER THANASIS WAS SELECTED BY THE NEW YORK KNICKS IN THE SECOND ROUND OF THE 2014 NBA DRAFT.

# Who was often referred to as the Human Highlight Film?

During the 1980s, the high-flying Michael Jordan took the NBA by storm. There was only one player who could stand toe-to-toe with Jordan when it came to throwing down dunks: Atlanta Hawks star **Dominique Wilkins**.

Wilkins was all about power. He would leap off of two feet, coming to a stop before unloading ferocious dunks, often his signature windmill. Those eye-popping slams earned him a fitting nickname: Human Highlight Film.

Wilkins was more than just a dunker, though. A nine-time All-Star, he was a skilled scorer who led the league in points per game (30.3) in 1985–86. In 2006, he was inducted into the Basketball Hall of Fame.

**FAST FACT**

NNEKA (2012) AND CHINEY ('14) EACH WON THE WNBA'S ROOKIE OF THE YEAR AWARD.

## Who were the only siblings to be drafted first overall?

Sisters **Nneka** and **Chiney Ogwumike** aren't twins, though their accomplishments on the basketball court have been nearly identical. They both played at Cypress-Fairbanks High School in Texas, where they each were named the Gatorade girls' basketball national player of the year (Nneka in 2008, Chiney in 2010). They both played for Stanford, where they were named Pac-12 Player of the Year twice (Nneka in 2010 and '12, Chiney in 2013 and '14).

They both were selected first overall in the WNBA draft — Nneka by the Los Angeles Sparks in 2012; Chiney by the Connecticut Sun in 2014. They're the only pair of siblings to each be drafted first overall in the NBA or WNBA drafts. On July 13, 2014, the siblings faced each other as opponents for the first time. Nneka led the Sparks to the win, scoring 24 points.

# Who was the dunking pioneer known as Chocolate Thunder?

**Darryl Dawkins** might have been the most powerful dunker in basketball history. Standing 7-feet tall and 250 pounds, he was famous for shattering the backboard with his thunderous dunks. Dawkins was known for one other thing: nicknames. His most famous one was Chocolate Thunder. Dawkins told *Dime* magazine that it was music legend Stevie Wonder who gave him that name. Dawkins also referred to himself as Sir Slam and Dr. Dunkenstein.

Dawkins was one of the first players to jump to the NBA straight from high school. After starring at Maynard Evans High School in Orlando, Florida, Dawkins was taken by the Philadelphia 76ers fifth overall in the 1975 draft. He spent 15 seasons in the NBA, most of them as a starter for the 76ers and then later the New Jersey Nets. However, injuries prevented him from becoming a star. His nicknames would become more famous than his play.

★ | SUPER STAT

# 386

PERSONAL FOULS DAWKINS COMMITTED IN 1983-84, A SINGLE-SEASON RECORD

# WHO TRADEMARKED HIS FAMOUS UNIBROW?

▶ The NBA has seen some crazy hairstyles. In **Anthony Davis** 's case, his signature style was not the hair on his head, but the thick patch between his eyebrows: his famous unibrow. That unique facial feature is far from the most interesting thing about Davis's physical stature. With his incredibly long arms (his wingspan was measured at 7' 4" before the draft), the 6' 10" Davis is one of the NBA's best young big men.

As a freshman at the University of Kentucky, Davis led the Wildcats to a national title. He was one of the most dominating defensive players in the history of the college game. Davis was named the Final Four's Most Outstanding Player despite scoring only six points in Kentucky's title game victory over Kansas. Over the two Final Four weekend games, Davis had 30 rebounds and 11 blocked shots.

The New Orleans Hornets, now known as the Pelicans, made Davis the top overall pick of the 2012 draft. In 2013–14, his second season in the league, he averaged more than 20 points and 10 rebounds a game and led the league in shot blocking (2.8 per game). He was also named an All-Star that year.

**FAST FACT**

DAVIS IS ONE OF FOUR FRESHMEN TO EVER WIN MOST OUTSTANDING PLAYER AT THE NCAA TOURNAMENT.

★ **SUPER STAT**

**19** YEARS OLD, DAVIS'S AGE WHEN HE WON GOLD WITH TEAM USA AT THE 2012 LONDON OLYMPICS, MAKING HIM THE YOUNGEST PLAYER TO EVER WIN OLYMPIC GOLD WITH USA MEN'S BASKETBALL

# Who was the only Australian-born player to win Rookie of the Year?

Dred Irving was a star at Boston University in the 1980s, finishing his career as the school's all-time leading scorer. He went on to play professionally with the Bulleen Boomers in Australia. While he was playing there in 1992, his wife gave birth to a son, Kyrie Irving.

The Irvings moved back to the U.S. when Kyrie was 2 years old. He was a top recruit for Duke University, and despite an injury-filled freshman year, he declared for the 2011 NBA draft. The Cleveland Cavaliers took him with the top pick. Irving shined for the Cavs in his first season. He led all rookies in scoring (18.5 points per game) and averaged a team-high 5.4 assists per game. He was named the NBA Rookie of the Year. Through the 2013–14 season, it was the only time the award had gone to a player born in Australia.

★ **SUPER STAT**

**20** YEARS OLD, IRVING'S AGE WHEN HE SCORED 41 POINTS AGAINST THE NEW YORK KNICKS, MAKING HIM THE YOUNGEST PLAYER TO EVER SCORE 40 AT NEW YORK'S MADISON SQUARE GARDEN

# Who was the shortest player to lead the NBA in rebounding?

Typically, the best rebounders are also the tallest players. But that was never the case with NBA legend **Charles Barkley**. He was known as the Round Mound of Rebound because of his unusual build: Depending on whom you believe, Barkley was somewhere between 6' 4" and 6' 6", meaning he was sometimes half a foot shorter than the players he was battling on the boards. He also had the kind of thick build you'd expect to see on a football field, not a basketball court.

So how is it that Barkley, in his third NBA season, became the shortest player to lead the NBA in rebounding when he grabbed 14.6 boards per game for the Philadelphia 76ers in 1986–87? For one, he was really strong. He easily cleared out space around the basket. He was also deceivingly athletic, with a feel for where missed shots would bounce. But most of all, he was tenacious. A young Barkley was a ball of energy, outworking taller players for all those boards. That season was anything but a fluke. During his 16-season Hall of Fame career, Barkley averaged double-digit rebounds 15 times.

**FAST FACT**

ALONG WITH STAR MICHAEL JORDAN, BARKLEY APPEARED IN THE 1996 LOONEY TUNES FILM SPACE JAM.

RECOR
BRE

LAKERS

★ THESE PLAYERS
CEMENTED THEIR PLACE
IN NBA HISTORY

# WHO SET THE NBA AND NCAA RECORDS FOR THREE-POINTERS MADE IN A SEASON?

▶ At the 2008 NCAA tournament, sophomore **Stephen Curry** led the underdog Davidson Wildcats to the Elite Eight, where they faced top-seeded Kansas. The Wildcats fell short against the eventual champions 59–57, but it was still a memorable night for Curry. The point guard scored a game-high 25 points, including his 159th three-pointer of the season, setting the NCAA single-season record.

A first-team All-America as a junior, Curry declared for the NBA draft in April 2009. He was an immediate star, playing his way onto the All-Rookie first team. On the final day of the 2012–13 season, he needed one three-pointer to tie Ray Allen's single-season record of 269. Curry hit four in that game, finishing the season with 272. Curry also shot with remarkable accuracy, making 45.3 percent of his shots from behind the arc that season. He was voted to his first All-Star Game in 2014 and named to the All-NBA second team.

★ | **SUPER STAT**

# 11

THREE-POINTERS MADE BY CURRY IN A 2013 GAME AGAINST THE NEW YORK KNICKS, A WARRIORS' SINGLE-GAME RECORD

# Who played in the most career NBA games?

## 10,117

DEFENSIVE REBOUNDS MADE BY PARISH IN HIS CAREER, RANKING FOURTH ON THE ALL-TIME LIST

When it comes to having a long and memorable NBA career, no one can top big man **Robert Parish**. Parish played in a record 1,611 games in a career that spanned 21 seasons and four championships. The 7' 1", 250-pound center was known for his defense and high-arcing jumper. He averaged double-digits in points for 17 straight seasons from 1977–78 through '93–94 and was a nine-time All-Star.

Parish is most remembered for his 14 seasons with the Boston Celtics. Parish and teammates Larry Bird and Kevin McHale were nicknamed the Big Three for their dominance, as they led the Celtics to titles in 1980–81, '83–84, and '85–86. (Parish's fourth championship came with the Chicago Bulls in the final season of his career.)

*HOLDSCLAW HAS A STREET NAMED AFTER HER IN KNOXVILLE, TENNESSEE.*

# Who set the WNBA record for rebounds in a game?

At 6' 2", **Chamique Holdsclaw** was not the biggest player — but she was the most imposing under the basket, leading the WNBA in rebounds in 2002 and '03. In the Washington Mystics' first game of the 2003 season, the forward grabbed 24 rebounds against the Charlotte Sting to break the WNBA record. She also scored 22 points to lead the Mystics to a 74–70 win.

A four-time All-America at the University of Tennessee, Holdsclaw led the Lady Vols to three consecutive NCAA championships (1996, '97, and '98). She was taken with the overall Number 1 pick by the Mystics in the 1999 WNBA draft. Holdsclaw went on to become the WNBA's scoring champion in 2002 and a six-time WNBA All-Star.

# Who broke the NBA mark for most points in one quarter?

On January 23, 2015, Golden State Warriors shooting guard **Klay Thompson** was unstoppable, scoring 52 points, with 11 three-pointers, to beat the Sacramento Kings 126–101. What he did in the third quarter was truly brilliant: He went 13 for 13 from the field, including nine three-pointers (the most ever in a quarter), and totalled a record-shattering 37 points in the period. A sharpshooter with a picture-perfect release, the 6'7" Thompson was the 11th overall pick in the 2011 NBA draft and named to the NBA All-Rookie First Team in 2012. He played in his first All-Star Game in 2015. Thompson and guard Stephen Curry formed the Warriors backcourt nicknamed Splash Brothers for their dazzling playmaking and amazing shooting abilities.

# 11

BLOCKED SHOTS MADE BY
GRINER ON JUNE 29, 2014
AGAINST THE TULSA SHOCK,
A WNBA SINGLE-GAME
RECORD

# WHO BROKE THE WNBA RECORD FOR BLOCKS IN A SEASON?

▶ **Brittney Griner** is an opponent's worst nightmare. At 6' 8" and 207 pounds, the center possesses a mix of size (she has an 88-inch wingspan and wears a size 17 shoe) and skill (her dunks are always highlight-worthy) that the game has never seen before. In addition to being an offensive force, she is dominant on the defensive end: In her first year in the WNBA, she led the league in blocks with 81, and she followed up that performance with a record-breaking sophomore campaign for the Phoenix Mercury. Her 129 shots blocked in 2014 shattered the previous mark of 114. In Game 3 of the 2014 WNBA Finals, she set a record for most blocks in a quarter. Only seven minutes into the first quarter, she made five blocks. Griner went on to break the Finals record with three more in the game.

Griner made a name for herself as a college star at Baylor. As a freshman, she swatted 6.4 shots per game and set an NCAA record for blocks in a season with 233. In 2011–12, she led the Lady Bears to the NCAA championship and was named the Final Four Most Outstanding Player. The top pick of the 2013 WNBA draft, Griner won her first WNBA title in 2014.

# Who had the most assists in a single game?

On December 30, 1990, Orlando Magic point guard **Scott Skiles** made history against the Denver Nuggets when he dished out a jaw-dropping 30 assists, the highest single-game total in NBA history. The 6' 1" point guard had more than twice as many assists as the Nuggets' team total (14). He also scored 22 points to lead the Magic to a 155–116 win.

Although Skiles was an NBA journeyman who never played in an All-Star Game, he left his mark. While at Michigan State, Skiles was the Big Ten Player of the Year in 1986. He was also the NBA's Most Improved Player in 1991 with the Magic. His basketball savvy allowed him to become a successful head coach after his playing days, leading the Phoenix Suns, Chicago Bulls, and Milwaukee Bucks.

★ **SUPER STAT**

**26** CONSECUTIVE GAMES IN WHICH THE CHICAGO BULLS HELD OPPONENTS BELOW 100 POINTS WITH SKILES AS THEIR COACH IN 2004-05, A FRANCHISE RECORD

# Who played in the most NBA All-Star Games?

You could make the argument that **Kareem Abdul-Jabbar** is the greatest to ever play the game. He is certainly the most decorated. No player in NBA history has ever scored more points (38,387), won more MVP awards (six), and made more All-Star appearances (19). Abdul-Jabbar also played the game with unmatched grace at the big man's position.

Born Lew Alcindor (Abdul-Jabbar changed his name before the 1971–72 season), he led the UCLA Bruins to three national titles and was a two-time National Player of the Year. The Milwaukee Bucks selected him with the first pick in the 1969 draft, and he was immediately the most imposing center in the league, winning Rookie of the Year honors his first season. After one NBA title and three MVP awards with the Bucks, Abdul-Jabbar was traded to the Los Angeles Lakers in 1975. He helped lead the Lakers to five championships. With his signature skyhook, Abdul-Jabbar changed the game and sealed his legacy as one of the NBA's all-time greats.

**FAST FACT**

ABDUL-JABBAR WAS NOT JUST AN OFFENSIVE FORCE. HE WAS A MEMBER OF THE NBA ALL-DEFENSIVE FIRST TEAM FIVE TIMES.

# WHO LED THE LEAGUE IN REBOUNDING THE MOST CONSECUTIVE SEASONS?

▶ With his crazy-colored hair and wild style, the 6' 7", 220-pound **Dennis Rodman** was always easy to spot on the court. But it would often seem like he was coming out of nowhere to crash the boards to grab rebound after rebound. Rodman had a knack for locating the ball once it was shot and outworked opponents, making him a seven-time NBA rebounding champion. He led the league in boards per game for seven consecutive seasons (1991–92 through 1997–98). His elite rebounding ability made Rodman a key part of five championship teams (the Detroit Pistons in 1989 and '90 and the Chicago Bulls in '96, '97, and '98). Legendary players Isiah Thomas and Michael Jordan stole the spotlight during those championship runs, but it was Rodman's hustle on both ends of the floor that helped those squads win titles. A two-time All-Star and seven-time member of the All-Defensive First Team, Rodman was also named the NBA Defensive Player of the Year twice (1989–90 and '90–91).

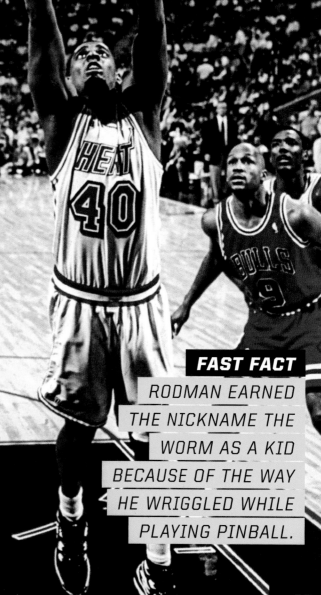

**FAST FACT**

RODMAN EARNED THE NICKNAME THE WORM AS A KID BECAUSE OF THE WAY HE WRIGGLED WHILE PLAYING PINBALL.

# Who had the most steals in one quarter?

With his dizzying ability to make smart plays and score, point guard **Lafayette "Fat" Lever** was a dangerous offensive player. But perhaps his biggest weapon was his pesky ability to steal. Over his career, he averaged 2.2 steals a game. His best pick-pocketing performance came on March 9, 1985. Lever had a triple double in that game (13 points, 15 assists, and 10 steals) to lead his Denver Nuggets to a victory over the Indiana Pacers. The highlight came in the third quarter, when he made eight steals, a record for most in a quarter.

Over the course of his 12-year career Lever also averaged 13.9 points, 6.2 assists, and 6.0 rebounds per game. He was a two-time NBA All-Star (1988 and '90) and made the All-NBA second team in 1987 and the All-Defensive second team in 1988.

**FAST FACT**

EATON BLOCKED 3,064 SHOTS AS A MEMBER OF THE UTAH JAZZ, A FRANCHISE RECORD.

# Who blocked the most shots in an NBA season?

Center **Mark Eaton** never averaged double-digit points per game during his 11-year career. But his focus was on the defensive end, where he will forever be remembered as one of the best rim protectors the NBA has ever seen. During the 1984–85 NBA season, he blocked 456 shots, an NBA record for most blocks in a season. Eaton blocked an amazing 5.6 shots per game that year. The 7' 4", 290-pound center spent his entire career as a member of the Utah Jazz. He was a two-time NBA Defensive Player of the Year (1984–85 and '88–89) and made the All-Defensive first team three times.

Eaton led the league in blocks four times in his career. He also was tops in the league in defensive rebounds in 1984–85 with 720.

# Who set the record for the most consecutive free throws made?

**Micheal Williams** of the Minnesota Timberwolves holds one of the most impressive streaks in NBA history. From March 24, 1993 though November 9, 1993, Williams made 97 consecutive free throws without a miss. He broke Houston Rockets point guard Calvin Murphy's previous mark of 78, set in 1981.

Williams played for Baylor University and was selected by the Detroit Pistons with the 48th pick of the 1988 draft. He spent only one season with the Pistons, but won an NBA title with them as a rookie. In addition to his free-throw streak, he finished in the top 10 in assists and steals in 1992–93.

★ | **SUPER STAT**

# 90.7

FREE-THROW PERCENTAGE BY WILLIAMS IN THE 1992-93 SEASON, THE FOURTH-BEST IN THE NBA THAT SEASON

**FAST FACT**

KORVER IS ALSO A RELIABLE FREE-THROW SHOOTER. IN 2006–07 HE LED THE LEAGUE WITH A .914 FREE-THROW PERCENTAGE.

# WHO BROKE THE RECORD FOR THE MOST CONSECUTIVE GAMES WITH A THREE-POINTER?

The three-pointer is the most valuable shot in basketball. And when it comes to making long-range shots, few have done it better than Atlanta Hawks swingman **Kyle Korver**. From November 2, 2012 through March 6, 2014, Korver hit at least one three-point field goal for an NBA record 127 straight games. He shattered the former streak of 89, set by Dana Barros (from December 23, 1994 to January 10, 1996). During the 127-game run, Korver made an astounding 337 threes. His Hawks teammate Jeff Teague put it best when he told the *New York Times*, "When Kyle is in the building, he is within range."

A star at Creighton University, Korver was a two-time Missouri Valley Conference Player of the Year. His 371 career three-pointers are sixth-best in NCAA history. Korver was taken in the second round of the 2003 draft by the New Jersey Nets, but was traded to the Philadelphia 76ers. While playing for the Sixers in 2004–05, he tied for the league lead with 226 three-pointers. The sharpshooter also finished with the highest three-point field goal percentage in 2009–10 and '13–14.

# 205

FREE THROWS MADE BY NOWITZKI IN THE 2006 PLAYOFFS, A RECORD FOR A SINGLE POSTSEASON

# Who made the most free throws without a miss in one game?

During the Dallas Mavericks' 2010–11 championship run, star big man **Dirk Nowitzki** was overpowering, with two 40-point performances and a 27.7 point-per-game average during the playoffs. Perhaps his most impressive feat came in Game 5 of the Western Conference finals against the Oklahoma City Thunder. Nowitzki went to the free-throw line 24 times — and made every shot, giving him the record for most free throws in a game without a miss. His cool at the line helped the Mavericks clinch the series and earn a spot in the NBA Finals. Led by Nowitzki, Dallas went on to upset the Miami Heat in six games, and Nowitzki took home the Finals MVP Award.

# Who set the mark for most consecutive games played?

The grind of playing basketball at such a high level takes a toll on a player, so missing games due to injury happens often. That is why **A.C. Green** 's feat of 1,192 consecutive games played is so impressive.

Green was a 6' 9" forward who averaged 9.6 points and 7.4 rebounds per game in his career. He was a three-time NBA champion as a member of the Los Angeles Lakers (1986–87, '87–88, '99–2000) and an All-Star in 1990. Green was a gritty player and tough defender. On November 20, 1997, Green played in his 907th consecutive game. It was the most ever at the time and he went on to play 285 more before finally sitting out on April 18, 2001. Green missed only three games his entire career, appearing in 1,278 of 1,281 games.

**FAST FACT**

*GREEN STARRED AT OREGON STATE UNIVERSITY, WHERE HE WAS A THREE-TIME MEMBER OF THE ALL-PAC-10 FIRST TEAM.*

★ | SUPER
STAT

# 9

SEASONS IN WHICH
STOCKTON LED THE
NBA IN ASSISTS

# WHO IS THE NBA'S CAREER LEADER IN ASSISTS?

▶ A point guard's job is to run the team's offense and make the players around him better. Few players in NBA history did that as well as **John Stockton**, the league's all-time assist leader. The Utah Jazz selected Stockton with the 16th overall selection in the 1984 NBA draft after being named the West Coast Conference Player of the Year as a senior at Gonzaga, averaging 20.9 points and 7.2 assists per game that season. When Stockton jumped to the NBA, his ability to see the floor was always on display. Stockton spent his entire career with the Jazz, and over the course of his 19 seasons in the NBA, he averaged 10.5 assists per game. In 1989–90, he had a career-high of 14.5 per game.

Stockton, a member of the original U.S. Dream Team that won gold at the 1992 Olympics, did most of his damage playing alongside one of the greatest forwards of all time, Karl Malone. On February 1, 1995, Malone received a bounce pass from Stockton and knocked down a baseline jumper. That assist helped Stockton surpass Magic Johnson as the NBA's all-time leader. Stockton didn't stop there. He finished his career with an astounding 15,806 assists before retiring after the 2002–03 season.

# Who had the highest free-throw percentage in a single season?

As a game-managing point guard always looking to make smart plays, **Jose Calderon** may not be the flashiest player. But he is quietly one of the NBA's most reliable shooters, especially from the free-throw line.

Calderon holds the single-season mark for best free-throw percentage. In 2008–09, his fourth year playing in the league, he shot a remarkable 98.1 percent from the line for the Toronto Raptors. From April 11, 2008 through January 30, 2009, Calderon made 87 consecutive free throws, the second longest streak in NBA history.

★ | **SUPER STAT**

# 3,770

ASSISTS MADE BY CALDERON AS A MEMBER OF THE TORONTO RAPTORS TO BECOME THE TEAM'S ALL-TIME LEADER IN THAT CATEGORY

# Who started off a game with the most consecutive three-pointers made?

Playing in a high-scoring, run-and-gun offense has its advantages for a point guard. Just ask **Ty Lawson**, who has the record for most three-pointers made to start a game. In 2010–11, the Denver Nuggets were the highest scoring team in the NBA with 107.5 points per game. Running that offense was the lightning-quick Lawson. On April 9, 2011, the Nuggets hosted the Minnesota Timberwolves. Lawson had a hot hand that day. He made his first 10 shots from three-point range to set a record for most consecutive three-pointers to start a game. Lawson finished with 37 points and led his Timberwolves to a 130–106 victory.

# Who blocked the most shots in a single game?

Los Angeles Lakers big man **Elmore Smith** gave one of the greatest defensive performances in NBA history on October 28, 1973, when he blocked 17 shots against the Portland Trail Blazers, setting a league record. He also tied the mark for most blocks in a half with 11. Swatting away the Blazers' shots, Smith helped the Lakers to a 111–98 win.

The 7' 0", 250-pound Smith was a force on both ends of the floor in his eight-year NBA career. He averaged a double-double in points and rebounds in his first five seasons in the league. The 13.8 rebounds per game that Smith averaged as a member of the Buffalo Braves, who later became the Los Angeles Clippers, is a franchise record. And in 1974 he led the NBA in blocks (393).

# WHO MADE THE MOST THREE-POINTERS IN NBA HISTORY?

▶ **Ray Allen** enjoyed a remarkable NBA career as one of the most accurate shooters in league history. A 10-time NBA All-Star and two-time NBA champion, Allen holds the NBA record for most career three-pointers, with an amazing 2,973 made heading into the 2014–15 season. (The previous record was 2,560, held by Indiana Pacers shooting guard Reggie Miller.)

Allen was a star at the University of Connecticut, setting the school's single-season scoring record. Even then, he had one of the prettiest jump shots in the game. With a quick release that allowed him to get his shot off even when a defender was rapidly approaching, Allen made shot after shot with a simple motion that stayed unchanged over the years. One reason Allen remained a scoring threat was his brilliance at using screens. Allen was very deceptive in the way he relied on his teammates to get himself open, time and time again, to do what he did best: sink a three.

**FAST FACT**

ALLEN WON THE NBA SPORTSMANSHIP AWARD IN 2003
AND HAS BEEN NAMED TO THE SPORTING NEWS' GOOD GUY
LIST THREE TIMES.

NBA All-Star Saturday Night

ALL·STAR

**FAST FACT**

IN 2004-05, HOWARD BECAME THE FIRST PLAYER TO JUMP
FROM HIGH SCHOOL TO THE NBA AND PLAY IN ALL 82 GAMES.

# WHO WAS THE TALLEST PLAYER TO WIN A SLAM DUNK CONTEST?

They say big guys never get respect in the NBA Slam Dunk contest because it's more exciting to see smaller players elevate and perform mid-air tricks. But with a 40-inch vertical leap, 6' 11" **Dwight Howard** could do all the things the little guys could, and then some. Before the 2008 contest, he came up with some of the most creative dunks the competition had ever seen. On one, Howard threw a toss from the left wing, leaped, tipped it off the backboard with his left hand, and then dunked it on the other side of the rim with his right.

But his signature dunk involved a costume. Howard took off his Orlando Magic jersey to reveal a Superman shirt, and he put on a red cape. He took off from just inside the free-throw line and soared so high up in the air that he threw the ball down through the hoop without touching the rim. He won the slam dunk title in a landslide, the tallest player ever to win it.

Howard's size, strength, and leaping ability make him the closest thing to a real-life Superman in the NBA. Those skills helped him become the first player to win the Defensive Player of the Year award three years in a row.

★ **SUPER STAT**

**5** CONSECUTIVE SEASONS IN WHICH HOWARD LED THE NBA IN TOTAL REBOUNDS (2005-06 TO '09-10), MAKING HIM THE ONLY PLAYER EVER TO ACHIEVE THAT FEAT

# SUPER
## SC

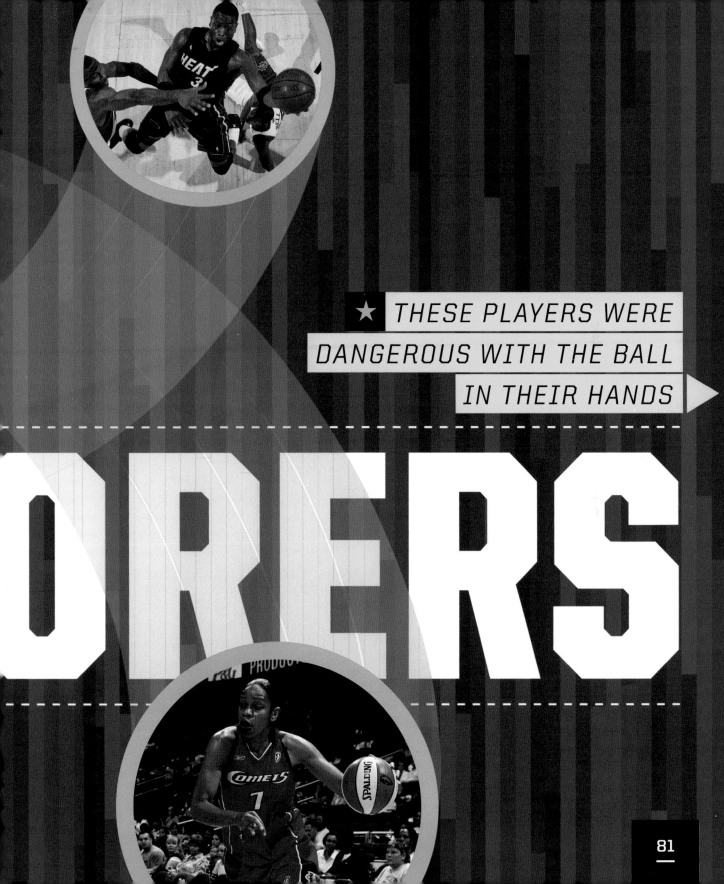

★ THESE PLAYERS WERE
DANGEROUS WITH THE BALL
IN THEIR HANDS

ORERS

# WHO SCORED THE MOST POINTS IN A GAME SINCE 1962?

▶ On January 22, 2006, the Los Angeles Lakers were trailing the Toronto Raptors by 17 points in the third quarter. Annoyed at his team's performance, **Kobe Bryant** took matters into his own hands. He scored 55 points, adding to the 26 he already had, leading the Lakers to a 122–104 comeback win. Bryant's 81 points were the most since March 2, 1962, when Philadelphia Warriors center Wilt Chamberlain scored 100 points against the New York Knicks. Bryant finished the game with 28 made field goals, going 7-for-13 on three-pointers and 18-for-20 on free throws.

Bryant was drafted by the Charlotte Hornets 13th overall in 1996, but a deal had already been reached to send him to the Lakers. Since Bryant was only 17 at the time, his parents had to sign his contract. In the years that followed, Bryant developed into one of the game's all-time greats, setting a record with 16 straight All-Star selections. He won five championships with the Lakers, earned Finals MVP honors in 2009 and '10, led the NBA in scoring twice, and was named to the All-Defensive First Team nine times.

**SUPER STAT**

# 35.4

POINTS PER GAME, BRYANT'S
AVERAGE IN 2005-06,
THE HIGHEST MARK
SINCE 1987

**FAST FACT**

KOBE IS A CITY IN JAPAN THAT LENDS ITS NAME TO A KIND OF BEEF.
BRYANT'S PARENTS WERE INSPIRED TO CHOOSE THE NAME KOBE
AFTER SEEING IT ON A RESTAURANT MENU.

# Who had the most 50-point games in NBA history?

**Wilt Chamberlain** scored 50 or more points in a game a whopping 118 times. Nobody else in NBA history has reached that mark even 40 times. Chamberlain famously had 100 points on March 2, 1962, breaking his own single-game record of 78. He finished that season with 45 games in which he scored 50 or more points.

Chamberlain's dominant scoring ability led to rule changes. When Chamberlain was a college freshman at Kansas (during an era when freshmen were generally not allowed to play on varsity teams), his scoring ability was already legendary. Chamberlain had a reputation for taking a running start and dunking his foul shots, an idea so terrifying to the rest of the college basketball world that it was outlawed before he even appeared in a game.

## FAST FACT

IN 1972, CHAMBERLAIN BECAME THE FIRST NBA PLAYER TO SCORE 30,000 CAREER POINTS. HE RETIRED A YEAR LATER WITH 31,419 POINTS.

★ **SUPER STAT**

# 3,070

CAREER REBOUNDS BY THOMPSON, THE ONLY WNBA PLAYER TO SCORE 7,000 POINTS AND PULL DOWN 3,000 BOARDS IN A CAREER

## Who is the WNBA's all-time leading scorer?

In her remarkable WNBA career, **Tina Thompson** racked up 7,488 points, the most in league history. After a stellar career at USC, Thompson was the first player taken in the first-ever WNBA draft, in 1997. Thompson won the first four WNBA championships with the Houston Comets, ultimately scoring 5,424 points in 12 seasons with the team. Thompson amassed another 1,327 points in three seasons for the Los Angeles Sparks, and added 737 in two years for the Seattle Storm before retiring in 2013. By that time, Thompson was also the WNBA's all-time leader in games played (496), ranked second in career rebounds (3,070), and had the tenth-most career blocks (372). The hard-working and well-respected Thompson will forever be known as a WNBA pioneer.

## Who has the highest career three-point field goal percentage?

Guard **Steve Kerr** was a prolific long-range shooter for 15 NBA seasons, retiring in 2003 having made 45.4 percent of his three-pointers. Kerr earned a reputation as an elite shooter in college at Arizona, where as a senior he shot 57.3 percent from deep.

In the NBA, Kerr was a valuable role player, winning five championships. He played for the Chicago Bulls during their title runs from 1996 to '98. In Game 6 of the 1997 Finals against the Utah Jazz, Kerr hit the championship-winning shot with five seconds left. After being traded in 1998 to the San Antonio Spurs, Kerr helped his new team to the 1999 title. He became the first player since the 1960s to win a championship in four straight seasons.

# WHO IS THE LAST GUARD TO WIN A SCORING TITLE?

► You don't earn the nickname Flash without lightning speed, and **Dwyane Wade**'s ability to drive and score was on full display in the 2008–09 season. With 30.2 points per game, he was the last guard to lead the NBA in scoring, getting most of his points in the paint and at the free-throw line.

Wade was the fifth pick in the 2003 draft.(He would've gone higher in most seasons, but future All-Stars LeBron James, Carmelo Anthony, and Chris Bosh went ahead of him.) By his third season, he was a superstar, leading the Miami Heat to its first-ever NBA title. Wade won Finals MVP honors in 2006 after averaging 34.7 points in a six-game series win over the Dallas Mavericks. He dominated, driving to the hoop and using his quickness and explosiveness to finish at the rim and draw fouls, earning 97 free-throw attempts in the Finals and making 75 of them.

Wade continued to play at a high level in the seasons that followed and remained one of the league's most daring players, seeming to risk injury with every acrobatic drive into the paint. His intense style of play helped bring two more championships to Miami, in 2012 and '13.

**SUPER STAT**

★

# 21

FREE-THROW MAKES BY WADE
ON 25 ATTEMPTS IN GAME 5
OF THE 2006 NBA FINALS,
A FINALS RECORD

## FAST FACT

IN 2008–09, WADE BECAME THE FIRST-EVER PLAYER TO HAVE 2,000 POINTS, 500 ASSISTS, 100 STEALS, AND 100 BLOCKS IN A SEASON. AT 6' 4", HE ALSO BECAME THE SHORTEST PLAYER IN NBA HISTORY TO BLOCK 100 SHOTS IN A SEASON.

# Who made the most free throws in NBA history?

With a tremendous ability to score in the low post and on midrange jumpers, forward Karl Malone was one of the greatest offensive players in NBA history. Malone retired second in career points (36,928). In 19 NBA seasons, he shot 13,188 free throws and made 9,787 of them. Those both stand as NBA records.

Malone played in college at Louisiana Tech, where he got the nickname Mailman for delivering on the court. The Utah Jazz drafted him 13th overall in 1985, teaming him with point guard John Stockton to form one of the greatest duos in NBA history. In 18 seasons together, Stockton and Malone ran the pick-and-roll to perfection. Malone averaged 25.4 points per game in that span, finishing in the top five in points per game from 1987–88 through '99–2000.

★ | SUPER STAT

## 36,374

POINTS SCORED BY MALONE FOR THE JAZZ, THE MOST ANY PLAYER HAS HAD FOR A SINGLE FRANCHISE

*McHALE WON BACK-TO-BACK SIXTH MAN OF THE YEAR AWARDS IN 1984 AND '85.*

# Who was the first player to shoot better than 60 percent from the field and 80 percent from the line in the same season?

In the 1986–87 season, Boston Celtics forward Kevin McHale made 60.4 percent of his field goal attempts and 83.6 percent of his free throws. McHale worked tirelessly to perfect his low-post moves, making him tough to stop when he caught the ball under the hoop. Former Detroit Pistons forward John Salley, a frequent opponent of McHale's, called guarding McHale on the low block a "torture chamber" for defenders. McHale finished his NBA career as a three-time champion and a seven-time All-Star.

# Who was the first WNBA player to score 50 points in a game?

Late in the 2013 season, the Tulsa Shock were already eliminated from playoff contention when they visited the San Antonio Stars. That didn't stop Shock guard Riquna Williams from giving it her all in a record-setting performance. In a 98–65 blowout win for Tulsa, Williams scored a WNBA-record 51 points, becoming the first WNBA player to score 50 points in a game. Williams made eight of 14 three-point attempts, went nine-for-nine from the free-throw line, and didn't commit a single turnover in her historic performance.

# WHO WAS THE LAST PLAYER TO LEAD THE NBA IN POINTS AND STEALS IN THE SAME SEASON?

▶ At 6' 0" tall, Philadelphia 76ers guard **Allen Iverson** was, inch-for-inch, one of the best players in NBA history. Despite his small stature relative to other players, Iverson led the league in points and steals per game in the 2000–01 and '01–02 seasons. By the end of his career, he had led the league in scoring four times and steals per game three times.

Iverson was drafted first overall by the 76ers in 1996, becoming the shortest Number 1 pick in NBA history. He was the 1997 Rookie of the Year, establishing himself as one of the league's best scorers and most pesky defenders. The Sixers steadily improved over his first five seasons, winning an Eastern Conference title in 2001. Iverson was MVP that season, with a league-leading 31.1 points and 2.5 steals per game. He is the shortest player to ever win MVP honors. He improved on both totals the following season, with 31.4 points per game and 2.8 steals per game, again leading the NBA in both categories.

**FAST FACT**

IVERSON IS THE LAST PLAYER TO SCORE 55 POINTS IN A PLAYOFF GAME, DOING SO AGAINST THE HORNETS IN A 2003 FIRST-ROUND MATCHUP.

# 55

CONSECUTIVE GAMES IN WHICH
TAURASI MADE A THREE-POINTER,
A WNBA RECORD SPANNING
THREE SEASONS
(2007 TO '09)

# Who had the most scoring titles in WNBA history?

Phoenix Mercury guard **Diana Taurasi** has been the WNBA's scoring champion a record five times. She set a WNBA record when she averaged 25.3 points per game in 2006 and won the scoring title for four straight seasons (2008 through '11).

Taurasi has been a superstar at every level, proving that she is one the greatest female basketball players of all time. She was a star college player at UConn, winning three national titles and two Naismith College Player of the Year awards. Taken by the Phoenix Mercury in the 2004 WNBA draft, Taurasi went on to win Rookie of the Year that season. She has only added to her hardware since, leading the Mercury to three WNBA titles (in 2007, '09, and '14) while winning Finals MVP twice.

# Who made the most free throws in a single quarter?

On December 23, 2005, New Jersey Nets guard **Vince Carter** capped off a 51-point performance by hitting 16-of-17 free throws in the fourth quarter of a 95–88 Nets win over the Miami Heat. He set an NBA record by making 16 foul shots in one quarter.

Carter was an electrifying athlete when he entered the league in 1998. His acrobatic and powerful dunks made him an instant fan favorite, earning him eight-straight All-Star Game selections. The well-rounded Carter was also a great shooter and passer. He entered the 2014–15 season ranked 30th all time in points and seventh in three-pointers.

**FAST FACT**

CARTER MADE EIGHT THREE-POINTERS IN ONE HALF OF A 2001 PLAYOFF GAME AGAINST THE PHILADELPHIA 76ERS, AN NBA RECORD.

★ **SUPER STAT**

# 41

CONSECUTIVE GAMES IN WHICH DURANT SCORED 25 OR MORE POINTS IN 2013-14, A SINGLE-SEASON RECORD

**FAST FACT**

IN 2012-13, DURANT BECAME THE YOUNGEST PLAYER TO SHOOT BETTER THAN 50 PERCENT FROM THE FIELD, 40 PERCENT ON THREE-POINTERS, AND 90 PERCENT ON FREE THROWS.

# WHO WON THE SCORING TITLE AND MVP AWARD IN 2013-14?

▶ Oklahoma City Thunder forward **Kevin Durant** had accomplished more by the age of 25 than most NBA players do in a career. After finishing second in MVP voting to LeBron James two seasons in a row, Durant broke through to win the 2013–14 MVP award. That season he led the NBA in scoring with 32 points per game.

As a freshman at the University of Texas, Durant made an immediate impression — he scored 20 points in only 22 minutes of a blowout win in his debut. Durant went on to average 25.8 points and 11.1 rebounds in his first and only NCAA season and became the first freshman to be consensus National Player of the Year. The Seattle SuperSonics made Durant the overall Number 2 pick of the 2007 NBA draft, and he won Rookie of the Year honors in 2007–08. Durant continued to excel as a versatile scorer after the Sonics moved to Oklahoma City and became the Thunder. His 30.1 points per game in 2009–10 gave him his first of four scoring titles. Since then, Durant has continued to cement his place as one of the most dynamic scorers in the league.

# WHO SCORED THE MOST POINTS IN A GAME AT MADISON SQUARE GARDEN?

▶ On January 24, 2014, the New York Knicks had lost five straight games leading into a home game against the Charlotte Bobcats. **Carmelo Anthony** arrived at Madison Square Garden quieter than usual, but his performance on the court that night was loud and clear: Anthony poured in 62 points, a team record and the most ever scored at the historic Garden. He made 23 of 35 field-goal attempts (good for 65.7 percent) in a 125–96 blowout.

Scoring feats were nothing new for Anthony. In his only college season at Syracuse, he set a Final Four freshman record with a 33-point game against Texas, on his way to earning Most Outstanding Player of the tournament and leading Syracuse to its first national title. Anthony quickly became an NBA star, becoming the third teenager to score 40 points in a game during his rookie year with the Denver Nuggets. At the 2012 Summer Olympics, he set a Team USA record with 37 points in a win over Nigeria.

★ | **SUPER STAT**

# 21

POINTS PER GAME, ANTHONY'S SCORING AVERAGE AS A 19-YEAR-OLD ROOKIE, THE HIGHEST EVER BY A TEENAGER

**FAST FACT**

THE CURRENT MADISON SQUARE GARDEN IS THE FOURTH VERSION THE BUILDING. OPENED IN 1968, IT IS KNOWN AS THE WORLD'S MOST FAMOUS ARENA.

# Who was the first WNBA player to lead the league in free-throw percentage and three-point percentage in the same season?

New York Liberty point guard **Becky Hammon** led the WNBA with a 95.1 percent free-throw shooting rate and 46.9 percent shooting from beyond the arc in 2003. A seven-time All-Star, she ranks second in WNBA history in career three-pointers (829), fourth in assists (1,708), and seventh in points (5,841).

After retiring in 2014, Hammon joined the San Antonio Spurs coaching staff, becoming the first female full-time assistant coach in NBA history. She had attended Spurs practices and film sessions while recovering from a knee injury in 2013. Spurs head coach Gregg Popovich said he was "confident her basketball IQ, work ethic and interpersonal skills will be a great benefit to the Spurs."

**FAST FACT**

AN ALL-AMERICA PLAYER AT COLORADO STATE, HAMMON LED THE RAMS TO THE SWEET 16 OF THE 1999 NCAA TOURNAMENT.

# 58

THREE-POINTERS MADE
BY MILLER IN THE
2000 PLAYOFFS,
AN NBA RECORD

## Who once scored eight points in nine seconds in a comeback playoff victory?

In Game 1 of the 1995 Eastern Conference semifinals against the New York Knicks at Madison Square Garden, the Pacers trailed by six points with 18.7 seconds left. Indiana threw an inbounds pass to guard **Reggie Miller**, who hit a three-pointer with 16.4 seconds left. Miller then stole the Knicks' inbounds pass, dribbled to get behind the arc, and hit another three to tie the game. After the Knicks missed two foul shots and a follow-up jumper, Miller got the rebound and was fouled. He calmly hit two free throws with 7.5 seconds left to give the Pacers a two-point lead. Knicks guard Greg Anthony fell down as time expired on New York's final possession, giving the Pacers an improbable 107–105 comeback victory.

## Who was the only player to lead the NCAA, NBA, and ABA in scoring?

**Rick Barry** had a scoring touch no matter where he played. He was the nation's leading scorer at the University of Miami in 1964–65, averaging 37.4 points. Then in 1966–67, he led the NBA in scoring with 35.6 points per game for the San Francisco Warriors. Barry also scored a league-high 34 points per game for the ABA's Oakland Oaks in 1968–69.

Barry shot free throws in a distinct old-fashioned, underhand style. He made 90 percent of his career NBA foul shots and led the NBA in free-throw shooting six times.

★ **SUPER STAT**

# 23

PLAYOFF GAMES IN WHICH JAMES HAS FINISHED WITH AT LEAST 30 POINTS, 10 REBOUNDS, AND FIVE ASSISTS, AN NBA CAREER RECORD

# WHO WAS THE YOUNGEST PLAYER TO REACH 20,000 CAREER POINTS?

▶ By the time **LeBron James** was a high school junior, he had already been on the cover of SPORTS ILLUSTRATED, was friendly with Michael Jordan, and was a celebrity in northern Ohio. His high school team attracted 4,000 fans per game, and NBA scouts and coaches considered him a surefire superstar. No player had ever received so much hype and attention at such a young age. In 2003, he became the youngest player ever taken first overall in the NBA draft, the first of many milestones to come.

In 2004, he became the youngest player to win Rookie of the Year and the youngest to score 40 points in a game. In his second year, he became the youngest player to score 2,000 points in a season. In his third season, he became the youngest All-Star Game MVP and the youngest player to have a triple double in the playoffs. During the 2012–13 season, and shortly after his 28th birthday, James became the youngest player to score 20,000 career points, reaching that mark more than a year younger than any other player in NBA history.

## FAST FACT

ENTERING THE 2015 PLAYOFFS, JAMES HAD AVERAGED 31.7 POINTS IN 14 ELIMINATION GAMES, THE HIGHEST AVERAGE AMONG PLAYERS WHO HAVE PLAYED IN FIVE OR MORE SUCH GAMES.

PLAYM

# AKERS

★ THESE PLAYERS WERE THE SPARKPLUGS TO THEIR TEAMS' SUCCESS

# WHO WAS THE FIRST PLAYER TO WIN THE SLAM DUNK CONTEST AND BE NAMED ROOKIE OF THE YEAR IN THE SAME SEASON?

► He was the Number 1 pick in 2009, but because of a left knee injury, **Blake Griffin** of the Los Angeles Clippers didn't make his regular-season debut until 2010. In his first NBA game, he scored 20 points and grabbed 14 rebounds against the Portland Trail Blazers. All season Griffin used his strength and leaping ability to dominate the paint. He finished the season with 22.5 points and 12.1 rebounds per game, tops among rookies, and was voted NBA Rookie of the Year.

For all of Griffin's great performances, the most memorable came at All-Star weekend. Competing in the Slam Dunk Contest on his home court, he clinched the title by leaping over a car, catching an alley-oop pass from teammate Baron Davis (who was peeking out through the sun roof), and throwing it down.

★ | SUPER STAT

# 27

CONSECUTIVE DOUBLE DOUBLES BY GRIFFIN IN 2010–11, THE LONGEST STREAK FOR A ROOKIE IN MORE THAN 40 SEASONS

**FAST FACT**

IN HIGH SCHOOL, GRIFFIN WAS COACHED BY HIS FATHER, TOMMY GRIFFIN. HE WON A STATE TITLE IN EACH OF HIS FOUR SEASONS.

# Who was the player depicted on the NBA logo?

In 1969, NBA commissioner J. Walter Kennedy decided the league needed a logo and hired a man named Alan Siegel to create it. Siegel went through hundreds of photos before he landed on the perfect one: Los Angeles Lakers guard **Jerry West** dribbling the ball up court. He made a drawing based on the photo — and the NBA had its logo.

Nicknamed Mr. Clutch, West was known for making big plays. He famously hit a 60-foot shot at the buzzer in Game 3 of the 1970 Finals, forcing overtime. The league introduced the Finals MVP award in '69, and even though West's Lakers lost to the Boston Celtics, he still won the award.

After his playing days and a brief stint in coaching, West went on to become a successful general manager for the Lakers and Memphis Grizzlies.

**FAST FACT**

*PARKER IS A TWO-TIME WINNER OF THE WOODEN AWARD AS COLLEGE BASKETBALL'S NATIONAL PLAYER OF THE YEAR.*

# Who was the first rookie to win WNBA MVP honors?

The Parkers are a basketball family. Larry Parker played at the University of Iowa. His son Anthony was a longtime pro player for the Toronto Raptors and Cleveland Cavaliers, among other teams. But the family's best basketball career belongs to his daughter, **Candace Parker**, an athletic 6' 4" center who can dunk with ease. As a junior and senior, she led the University of Tennessee to back-to-back NCAA titles, in 2007–08 and '08–09.

The Los Angeles Sparks made Parker the first overall pick of the 2008 WNBA draft. Teaming with future Hall of Famer Lisa Leslie, she took the Sparks back to the playoffs. Parker averaged 18.5 points, a league-leading 9.5 rebounds, and 2.3 blocks in her first season. Just months after winning an NCAA championship, she was named WNBA MVP, the first rookie to win the award.

# Who set the NBA's rookie record for three-pointers in a season?

Going into the 2012–13 season, no one knew what to expect from **Damian Lillard**, a point guard out of tiny Weber State. It was a big jump from a small college to the NBA, but it didn't take long for Lillard to make his mark. Starting in the season-opener for the Portland Trail Blazers, he used a combination of quickness and long-range shooting to have 23 points and 11 assists in an upset of the Los Angeles Lakers.

Even though he made only one three-pointer in that game, marksmanship would prove to be Lillard's greatest strength. He made 185 three-pointers that season, breaking Golden State Warriors guard Stephen Curry's record for three-pointers made by a rookie.

The following season, Lillard made 218 threes, averaging 20.7 points per game, as he and big man LaMarcus Aldridge helped the Blazers win their first playoff series in 14 years.

★ SUPER STAT

**3** PLAYERS WHO HAD AT LEAST 20 POINTS AND 10 ASSISTS IN THEIR FIRST NBA GAME: LILLARD AND HALL OF FAMERS OSCAR ROBERTSON AND ISIAH THOMAS

# WHO HAS LED THE LEAGUE IN STEALS THE MOST TIMES?

▶ To be a great point guard in the NBA, you need to be fast and smart. Point guards are quarterbacks on the court. They not only need to know where their teammates are at any given moment, but also where their opponents are as well.

That's what makes **Chris Paul** one of the best offensive point guards in NBA history. Along with the quickness to blow by defenders, he's great at anticipating how a defense will react to his moves, and how those reactions will lead to points for him or open shots for his teammates.

That high IQ is also what makes Paul one of the best defensive point guards ever to play the game, despite the fact that he's only 6-feet tall. Paul's quickness, smarts, and relentless energy allow him to smother opposing point guards.

Paul has led the NBA in steals a record six times in his first nine seasons (2005–06 through '13–14). Playing for the New Orleans Hornets, he led the league in steals per game in back-to-back years (2.7 in '07–08 and 2.8 in '08–09), and one more time in '10–11 (2.4 per game). He joined the Los Angeles Clippers the following season, and proceeded to lead the league in steals per game in each of his first three seasons in L.A.

★ SUPER STAT

**3** TIMES THAT PAUL HAS LED THE NBA IN ASSISTS PER GAME, INCLUDING A CAREER-HIGH 11.6 ASSISTS IN 2007-08

**FAST FACT**

PAUL IS AN AVID BOWLER. HE HAS A CAREER-HIGH SCORE OF 256 AND IS AN OFFICIAL SPOKESMAN FOR THE UNITED STATES BOWLING CONGRESS.

# Who was the first four-time Defensive Player of the Year winner?

**Dikembe Mutombo** may have the most famous celebration in the history of the hardwood. But he didn't do it when he scored a basket — he did it when he prevented one.

A 7' 2" center from the Congo, Mutombo was a prolific shot blocker. Every time he blocked a shot, he celebrated by wagging his index finger as if to say, "No you don't!" Selected fourth overall by the Denver Nuggets in the 1991 draft, Mutombo led the league in shot blocking three straight seasons from 1993–94 to '95–96. His defensive dominance made him the first four-time Defensive Player of the Year in league history ('94–95, '96–97, '97–98, and 2000–01). He won the awards with three different teams: the Nuggets, Atlanta Hawks, and Philadelphia 76ers.

**FAST FACT**

MUTOMBO IS KNOWN FOR HIS HUMANITARIAN WORK IN AFRICA. HE BUILT A HOSPITAL IN KINSHASA, THE CAPITAL OF HIS HOME COUNTRY OF THE CONGO.

# Who was the first three-time Slam Dunk Contest champion?

Even at 5' 9", Nate Robinson was a star on the hardwood with a 43.5-inch vertical leap. He put that leaping ability to good use in the NBA's Slam Dunk Contest. In 2006, he beat Andre Iguodala in the first-ever "Dunk Off." Robinson won it again in 2009 when he came out dressed in a green Knicks uniform and holding a glowing green basketball. He called himself "Krypto-Nate," a play on kryptonite, the fictional substance known as Superman's only weakness. And then he dunked over Superman. (Dwight Howard stood in front of the basket wearing a red cape.) The jaw-dropping performance all but clinched Robinson's second Slam Dunk title.

A year later, his double-pump reverse dunk in the finals gave Robinson a narrow victory over DeMar DeRozan, making him the first three-time Slam Dunk champion.

# Who was the only player in NBA history to average a triple double for a season?

The NBA has had no shortage of "do-it-all" superstars who pile up triple doubles (having double-digit statistics in three categories). But no one can match the feats of Oscar Robertson. Known as "The Big O," Robertson was a strong 6' 5" guard who simply overpowered opponents on the floor. Playing for the Cincinnati Royals and the Milwaukee Bucks (with whom he won an NBA title), Robertson had 181 career triple doubles. No one has come close to that record. Even more amazing was his performance for the Royals in 1961–62. That season he *averaged* a triple double: 30.8 points, 12.5 rebounds, 11.4 assists. It's a feat the basketball world had never seen before and will likely never see again.

# WHO WAS THE FIRST CANADIAN PLAYER TO WIN NBA MVP?

▶ Growing up in Victoria, British Columbia, Canada, **Steve Nash** didn't play basketball until he was about 12 years old. It's been quite a rise for the NBA star ever since. Nash started his career as an exciting, young point guard for the Phoenix Suns and the Dallas Mavericks, but it wasn't until he returned to Phoenix as a free agent, before the 2004–05 season, that he took his game to the next level.

Surrounded by rising young stars, and directing an exciting, fast-paced offense, Nash averaged a league-leading 11.5 assists per game, made 50.2 percent of his field goal attempts, and 43.1 percent of his threes. More importantly, with Nash leading the way, the Suns improved by a whopping 33 wins (from 29–53 to 62–20). After missing the playoffs the previous year, Phoenix finished with the best record in the NBA. Nash was named MVP, the first Canadian player to take home that award. A year later, Nash did it again. In 2005–06, he led the league in assists (10.5 per game) and free-throw percentage (92.1), joining Magic Johnson as the only point guards to win back-to-back NBA MVP awards.

**FAST FACT**

NASH GREW UP IN CANADA, BUT HE WAS BORN IN JOHANNESBURG, SOUTH AFRICA, WHERE HE LIVED UNTIL HE WAS 18 MONTHS OLD.

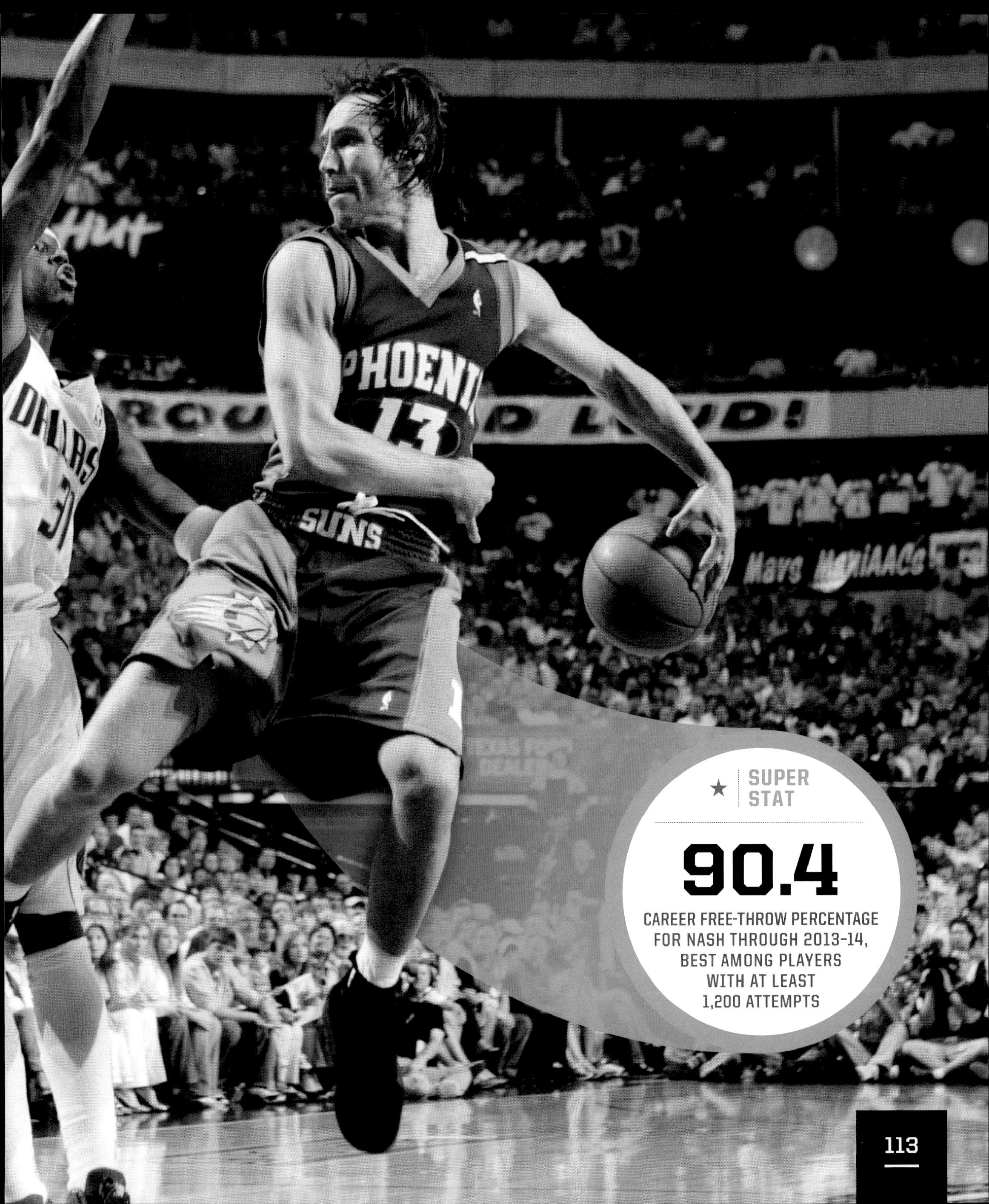


★ SUPER STAT

# 90.4

CAREER FREE-THROW PERCENTAGE FOR NASH THROUGH 2013-14, BEST AMONG PLAYERS WITH AT LEAST 1,200 ATTEMPTS

# WHO WAS THE LAST PLAYER TO HAVE A 20-ASSIST TRIPLE DOUBLE IN THE PLAYOFFS?

▶ Point guard **Rajon Rondo** has emerged as one of the top guards in the league. A player with super quickness, long arms, and a knack for setting up teammates with easy shots, Rondo was a key part of the Boston Celtics' 2008 championship run. By the time the 2011 playoffs came along, he was arguably the Celtics' best player. During a first-round playoff game against the New York Knicks, he filled up the stat sheet: 15 points, 11 rebounds, and a whopping 20 assists. It was the first time in 20 years that a player had a triple double that included 20 or more assists in a playoff game.

Rondo, who was traded to the Dallas Mavericks midway through the 2014–15 season, has a habit of coming up with big games in the playoffs. Through the 2014 postseason, there were only two active players who had recorded 10 or more playoff triple doubles during their career: LeBron James and Rondo.

**FAST FACT**

OFF THE COURT, ONE OF RONDO'S FAVORITE HOBBIES IS ROLLER-SKATING.

★ | **SUPER STAT**

**37** CONSECUTIVE GAMES WITH 10 OR MORE ASSISTS FOR RONDO TO START THE 2012-13 SEASON, TIED FOR THE SECOND-LONGEST STREAK OF ALL TIME

# Who won the most WNBA Defensive Player of the Year Awards?

**Tamika Catchings** was finishing a great career at the University of Tennessee when she tore the ACL in her right knee. Even though she had to sit out for an entire season, the Indiana Fever still selected her third overall in that year's draft. It was a risk, but it paid off.

Catchings was the league's Rookie of the Year and an All-Star in 2002. She made the All-Star team nine times through 2014. She also won the WNBA MVP award in 2011 and led the Fever to a title in 2012.

Catchings is not just a great offensive player. She has won five Defensive Player of the Year awards, more than any player in league history. She has also led the WNBA in steals per game six times and is the all-time leader in career steals (957 through 2014).

★ | SUPER STAT

# 1,773

CAREER FREE THROWS MADE BY CATCHINGS THROUGH THE 2014 SEASON, TOPS IN THE WNBA

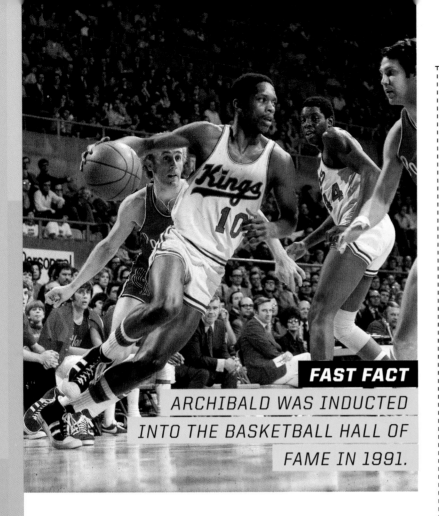

ARCHIBALD WAS INDUCTED INTO THE BASKETBALL HALL OF FAME IN 1991.

## Who was the youngest guard to finish with a triple double in an NBA game?

If there's one thing **John Wall** is known for, it's speed. Since the Washington Wizards made him the first overall pick of the 2010 draft, Wall has blown by opponents.

Considering how fast he works, it's no surprise that Wall pulled off great performances so early in his career. On November 10, 2010, Wall carried the Wizards to a win over the Houston Rockets with 19 points, 10 rebounds, and 13 assists. It was his sixth NBA game, and he was only 20 years, 65 days old at the time. It made him the youngest guard to ever have a triple double in an NBA game, and the third-youngest player of any position to pull off the feat.

## Who was the only player to lead the NBA in scoring and assists in the same season?

Point guards usually fall into one of two categories: scorers who pile up points or playmakers who set up their teammates. In 1972–73, Kansas City-Omaha Kings point guard **Nate (Tiny) Archibald** filled both roles, and did something no player had done before or since.

Archibald tore up opposing defenses, averaging an NBA-leading 34.0 points per game. But he didn't forget about his teammates. Archibald handed out a remarkable 11.4 assists per game, also tops in the league. He's the only player to ever lead the NBA in both of those categories in the same season. Archibald later won an NBA title with the Boston Celtics in 1980–81.

**FAST FACT**

THE FIFTH OVERALL SELECTION OF THE 1995 DRAFT, GARNETT WAS THE FIRST PLAYER TO BE DRAFTED DIRECTLY OUT OF HIGH SCHOOL IN 20 YEARS.

**4** TIMES GARNETT WAS NAMED NBA PLAYER OF THE MONTH IN 2003-04, THE FIRST INSTANCE IN WHICH A PLAYER HAD WON THE AWARD FOUR TIMES IN ONE SEASON

# WHO WAS THE LAST PLAYER TO LEAD THE LEAGUE IN REBOUNDING FOUR STRAIGHT SEASONS?

▶ The Minnesota Timberwolves took a big chance on draft night in 1995. The franchise had never won 30 games in a season, let alone competed for a playoff spot. It needed a star. And it found one in a high school player from Chicago named **Kevin Garnett** .

It wasn't long before Garnett brought respectability to the T-Wolves. In just his second season, he lifted them to the playoffs for the first time. He was big (6' 11") and a skilled athlete who was a force on defense. His intensity allowed him to become one of the greatest players ever on that end of the court. Garnett led the NBA in rebounding four straight seasons, from 2003–04 (when he was the league's MVP) through '06–07. He is the last player to win the rebounding crown in four consecutive seasons.

Despite some great years, the Timberwolves could never break through in the tough Western Conference. Garnett was traded to the Boston Celtics before '07–08 and, along with Paul Pierce and Ray Allen, helped the Celtics win an NBA championship.

# WHO WAS THE YOUNGEST PLAYER TO WIN THE NBA MVP AWARD?

▶ Before the 2010–11 season started, young Chicago Bulls point guard **Derrick Rose** had a question for the basketball world: "Why can't I be the MVP of the league?"

The obvious answer was that Rose was only 22 years old. No one had ever won the NBA's MVP award before the age of 23 (and that was more than 40 years ago, when Wes Unseld of the Baltimore Bullets won the award in 1968–69).

But Rose took his game to a new level in his third NBA season. He was already one of the most explosive guards in the league when it came to attacking the basket, and he was a smart point guard who made his teammates better. That year, he added a greatly improved jump shot, averaging a career-high 25 points to go along with 7.7 assists per game. More importantly, he made the Bulls a title contender. With an improved Rose leading the way, they finished with an NBA-best record of 62–20.

Rose answered his own question and beat out Orlando's Dwight Howard, Miami's LeBron James, Kobe Bryant of the Los Angeles Lakers, and Oklahoma City's Kevin Durant to become the youngest ever to take home league MVP.

**FAST FACT**

ROSE WON TWO ILLINOIS HIGH SCHOOL TITLES AT SIMEON CAREER ACADEMY IN CHICAGO, THE SAME SCHOOL MILWAUKEE BUCKS FORWARD JABARI PARKER ATTENDED.

★ **SUPER STAT**

**36** POINTS SCORED BY ROSE AGAINST THE BOSTON CELTICS IN GAME 1 OF THEIR 2009 PLAYOFF SERIES, TYING AN NBA ROOKIE RECORD FOR POINTS IN A DEBUT PLAYOFF GAME

# Who set the single-game playoff record for offensive rebounds?

**Moses Malone** 's game was all about second chances. The 6' 10" big man was drafted by the American Basketball Association's Utah Stars straight out of high school in 1974. As a 19-year-old rookie, he averaged 18.8 points and 14.6 rebounds.

When the ABA folded, Malone landed with the Houston Rockets and then the Philadelphia 76ers. He was nearly unstoppable. Part of it was his strength and skill in the low post, but most of it was his relentless work grabbing offensive rebounds. The ABA started tracking offensive rebounds in '67–68, and the NBA in '73–74. In the record books for most offensive rebounds in a single season, Malone is first (587 in '78–79), second (573 in '79–80), and third (558 in '81–82).

**FAST FACT**

*LESLIE WAS NAMED THE WNBA DEFENSIVE PLAYER OF THE YEAR IN 2004 AND '08.*

# Who was the first player to dunk in a WNBA game?

Women's basketball had never had a player quite like **Lisa Leslie** . A strong, skilled and athletic center, Leslie starred at the University of Southern California and Team USA (she won four Olympic gold medals, and her 35 points against Japan in the semifinals of the 1996 Olympic semifinals is a Team USA women's scoring record). When the WNBA started in 1996, Leslie joined her hometown Los Angeles Sparks and went on to win the league MVP award three times and lead L.A. to two WNBA titles.

But for all her accomplishments, Leslie might be best known for a single play during a game in 2002. Trying to come back against the Miami Sol, she sprinted up the court and received a long pass. Leslie took two dribbles, elevated, and stuffed it through the rim with her right hand, the first dunk in WNBA history.

# Who was the last player to have 50 consecutive double doubles?

From the moment he stepped on an NBA court, **Kevin Love** has been a rebounding and scoring machine. With a thick, muscular build and great instincts for how a ball is going to bounce off the rim, he's an elite rebounder. But unlike a lot of bruising big men, Love has a finesse game when it comes to scoring. He's such a good three-point marksman that he won the NBA's three-point shootout in 2012.

With a rare combination of skills, the double doubles piled up. In his first season as a regular starter, 2010–11, Love averaged 20.2 points per game and a league-leading 15.2 rebounds per game. Perhaps more impressively, he had a streak of 53 consecutive games with a double double. It was the longest streak the NBA has seen since the league merged with the American Basketball Association in 1976.

Love now puts those skills to use alongside LeBron James and Kyrie Irving in Cleveland, giving the Cavaliers one of the most exciting trios in the NBA.

★ SUPER STAT

## 31
POINTS AND REBOUNDS BY LOVE AGAINST THE NEW YORK KNICKS ON NOVEMBER 12, 2010, MAKING HIM THE 19TH PLAYER IN NBA HISTORY TO HAVE A 30-30 GAME

★ | **SUPER STAT**

# 9

STEALS CARTER-WILLIAMS MADE IN AN UPSET OF THE DEFENDING CHAMPION MIAMI HEAT ON OCTOBER 30, 2013, THE MOST EVER BY A PLAYER IN HIS NBA DEBUT

# WHO WERE THE ONLY ROOKIES TO HAVE A TRIPLE DOUBLE IN THE SAME GAME?

▶ In 2013, the Orlando Magic's **Victor Oladipo** and the Philadelphia 76ers' **Michael Carter-Williams** were both big rookie guards who could score, set up teammates, and play defense.

Their do-it-all skills were on display when the Magic visited the Sixers that December. The game was thrilling, with Orlando tying the game on a three-pointer with 18 seconds left. As the teams headed to overtime, Carter-Williams had 20 points, 11 rebounds, and six assists; Oladipo had 22 points, nine rebounds, and nine assists.

Their big performances continued in the first overtime. Oladipo reached 10 assists, while Carter-Williams finished the first OT with eight. The game went into *double* overtime and with 10 seconds left in the second OT, Oladipo grabbed his 10th rebound. It marked the first time that two rookies had a triple double in the same game.

The final stats: Oladipo had 26 points, 10 rebounds, and 10 assists. Carter-Williams had 27 points, 12 rebounds, and 10 assists to lead Philly to a 126–125 victory.

## FAST FACT

CARTER-WILLIAMS WON THE 2013–14 NBA ROOKIE OF THE YEAR AWARD. OLADIPO WAS SECOND IN THE VOTING.

# ▶ PLAYER INDEX

## L

Lawson, Ty, 75
Leslie, Lisa, 122
Lever, Fat, 66
Lieberman, Nancy, 45
Lillard, Damian, 107
Love, Kevin, 123

## M

Malone, Karl, 88
Malone, Moses, 122
McHale, Kevin, 89
Meyers, Ann, 39
Mikan, George, 16
Miller, Cheryl, 21
Miller, Reggie, 99
Ming, Yao, 42
Muresan, Gheorghe, 34
Mutombo, Dikembe, 110

## N

Nash, Steve, 112
Nowitzki, Dirk, 70

## O

Ogwumike, Chiney, 48
Ogwumike, Nneka, 48
Oladipo, Victor, 124
Olajuwon, Hakeem, 20
O'Neal, Shaquille, 10

## P

Parish, Robert, 58
Parker, Candace, 106
Parker, Tony, 6
Paul, Chris, 108
Payton, Gary, 38
Pierce, Paul, 26

## R

Robertson, Oscar, 111
Robinson, David, 24
Robinson, Nate, 111
Rodman, Dennis, 64
Rondo, Rajon, 114
Rose, Derrick, 120
Russell, Bill, 8

## S

Skiles, Scott, 62
Smith, Elmore, 75
Stockton, John, 72
Swoopes, Sheryl, 36

## T

Taurasi, Diana, 92
Thompson, Klay, 59
Thompson, Tina, 85
Thomas, Isiah, 16

## W

Wade, Dwyane, 86
Wall, John, 117
Walton, Bill, 18
Walton, Luke, 18
Webb, Spud, 44
Webber, Chris, 39
West, Jerry, 106
Westbrook, Russell, 40
Wilkins, Dominique, 48
Williams, Micheal, 67
Williams, Riquna, 89
Worthy, James, 21

# ▶ PHOTO CREDITS